T0063617

SWEARY CATS

Pavilion
An imprint of HarperCollins*Publishers* Ltd
1 London Bridge Street
London SE1 9GF

www.harpercollins.co.uk

HarperCollins*Publishers*
Macken House,
39/40 Mayor Street Upper,
Dublin 1
D01 C9W8

10 9 8 7 6 5 4 3 2 1

First published in Great Britain by
Pavilion, an imprint of HarperCollins*Publishers* 2023

Copyright © Pavilion 2023
Text © Andrew Davies 2023
Andrew Davies asserts the moral right to be identified as the author of this work. A catalogue record of this book is available from the British Library

ISBN 978-0-008589-02-8

This book is produced from independently certified FSC™ paper to ensure responsible forest management.

For more information visit:
www.harpercollins.co.uk/green

Printed and bound in China by RR Donnelley, APS

All rights reserved. No part of this publication may be reproduced, stored in a retrieval system, or transmitted, in any form or by any means, electronic, mechanical, photocopying, recording or otherwise, without the prior permission of the publishers.

This book is sold subject to the condition that it shall not, by way of trade or otherwise, be lent, re-sold, hired out or otherwise circulated without the publisher's prior consent in any form of binding or cover other than that in which it is published and without a similar condition including this condition being imposed on the subsequent purchaser.

SWEARY CATS

ANDREW DAVIES

PAVILION

Despicable Meow

"Cats have a scam going. You buy the food, they eat the food, they go away. That's the deal." Not my words, but those of Eddie Izzard describing her relationship with cats in a classic stand-up routine. Many think that cats are empathetic pets, uber cool, aware of people's feelings, who will nuzzle up when their owner is tearful and lick away their tears. Or maybe they just want the salt. Or maybe it's a health check to make sure the person who opens the moist pouches will still be available to open the next one in the cupboard. That vigorous rubbing at the back of the calves doesn't come from a spontaneous outburst of emotion, it happens at meal times. Dogs, on the other hand, want to be your best friend all the time. Dogs want to help you, guard you, fetch things (provided the thing is a stick or a heavily salivated tennis ball). Cats want to get on with their lives. They have their own

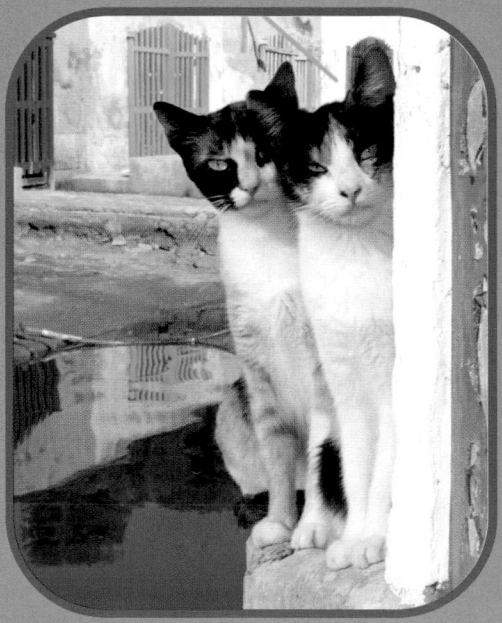

agenda, and if you interrupt it, they are seriously annoyed. They'll tolerate being picked up, but not for long. This book articulates some of the thoughts that run through a cat's mind when that happens, from the mildly hissed off; such as Martin, who's watching his favourite *Bagpuss* episode; to Abigail, who can't work out where the ginger kitten came from in her litter. Cats can be very cruel in both deed and word. Think of the two Siamese cats in the original, animated *Lady and the Tramp*: to Aunt Sarah they are her darling, pedigree pussies who can do no wrong. The minute her back is turned they wreak havoc in the house and stick the blame on someone else. That's what cats are like. They don't need to look like 'Zara – the cat with the cloak made from her enemy's fur' to be angry and vengeful. They don't need to give you an unblinking green-eyed stare to know that they are calculating and manipulative. They are cats – this is their bag. Welcome to their world...

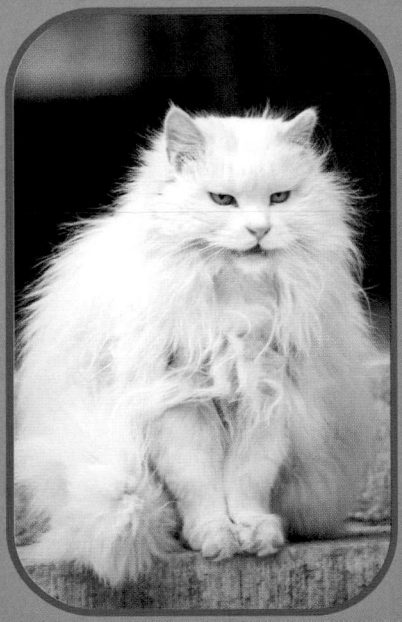

Andrew Davies

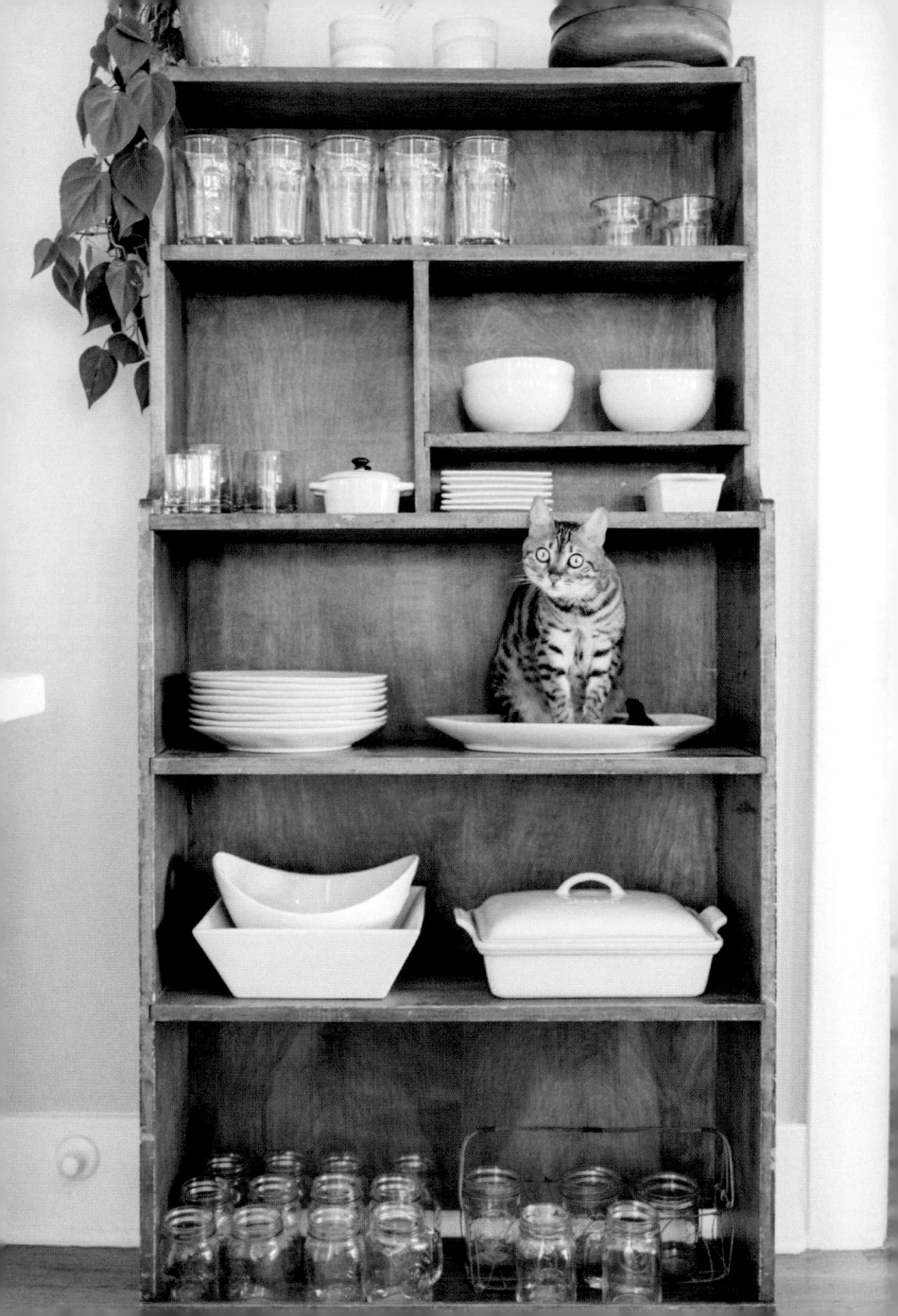

Yes! As a matter of fact I HAVE wiped my arse on ALL of your fucking crockery

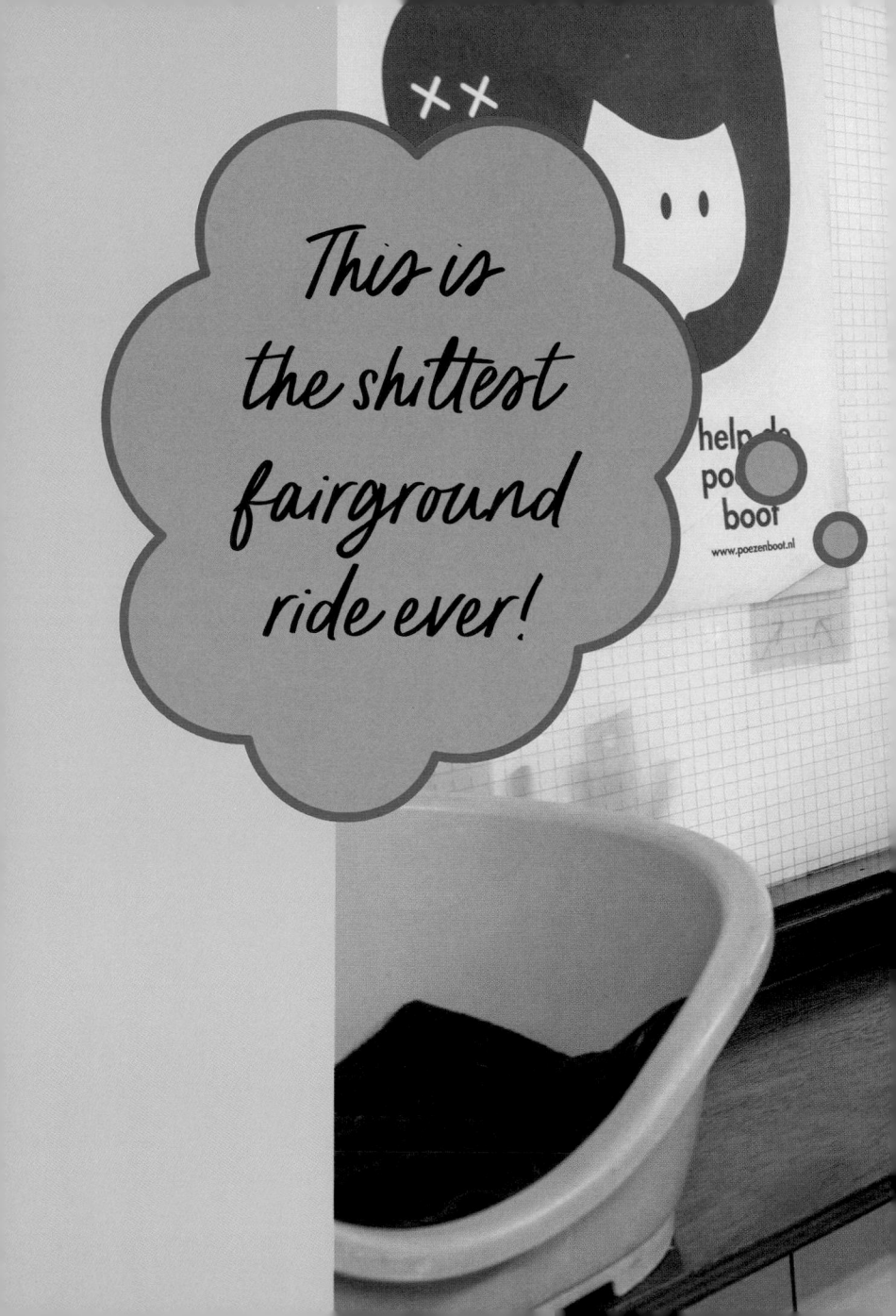
This is the shittest fairground ride ever!
help de
po
boot
www.poezenboot.nl

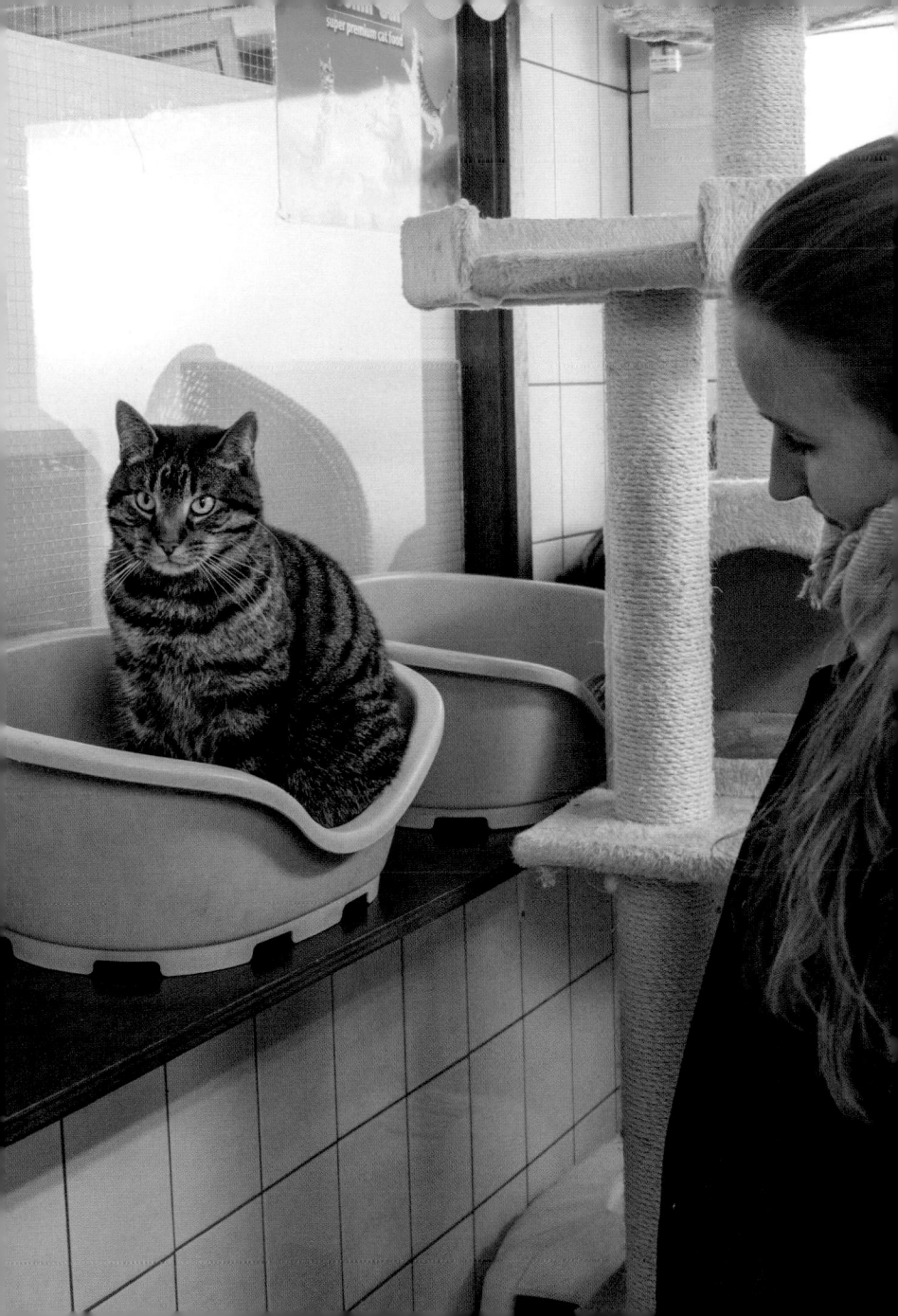
super premium cat food

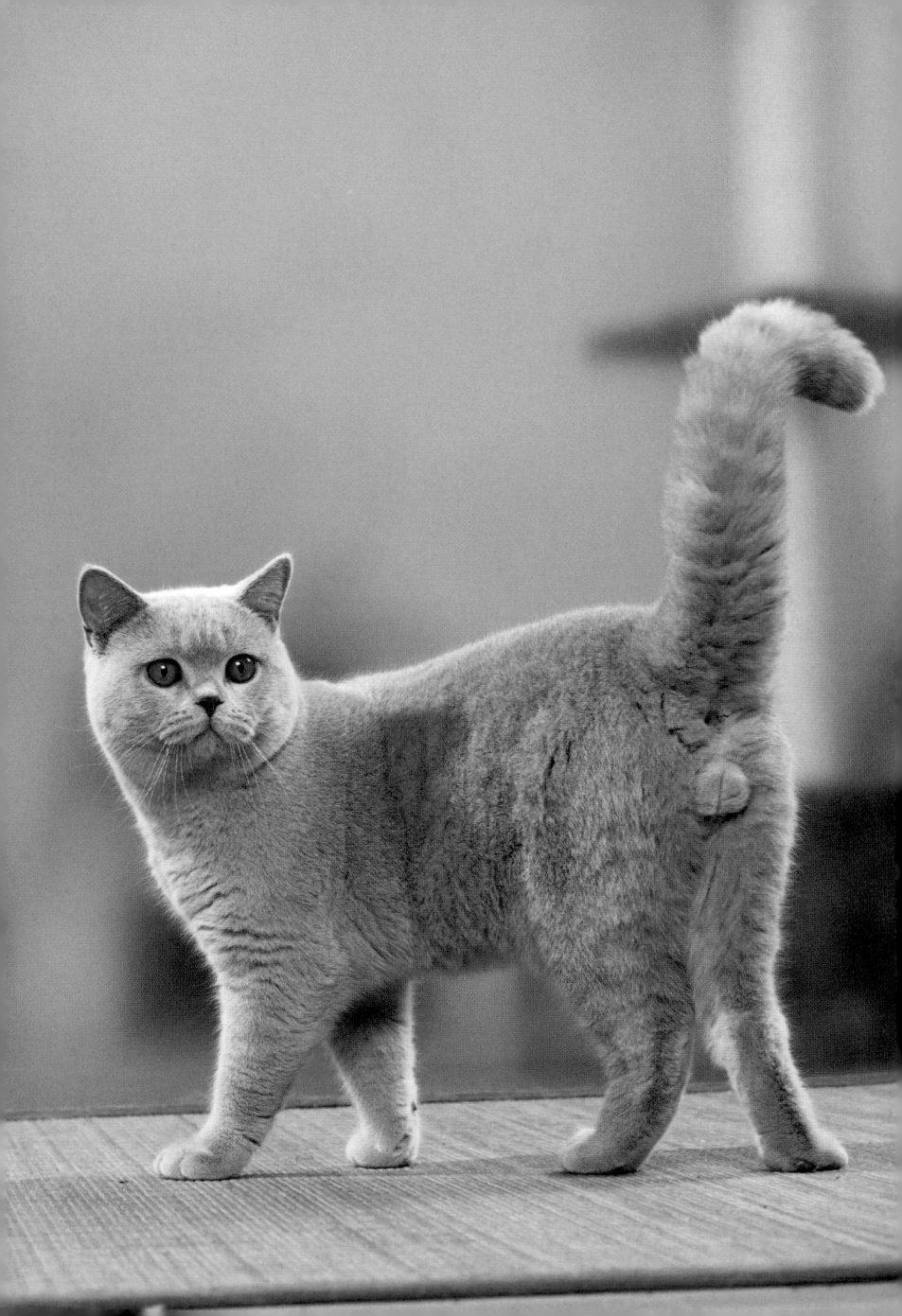

Erm, did I just hear someone mention THE SNIP?

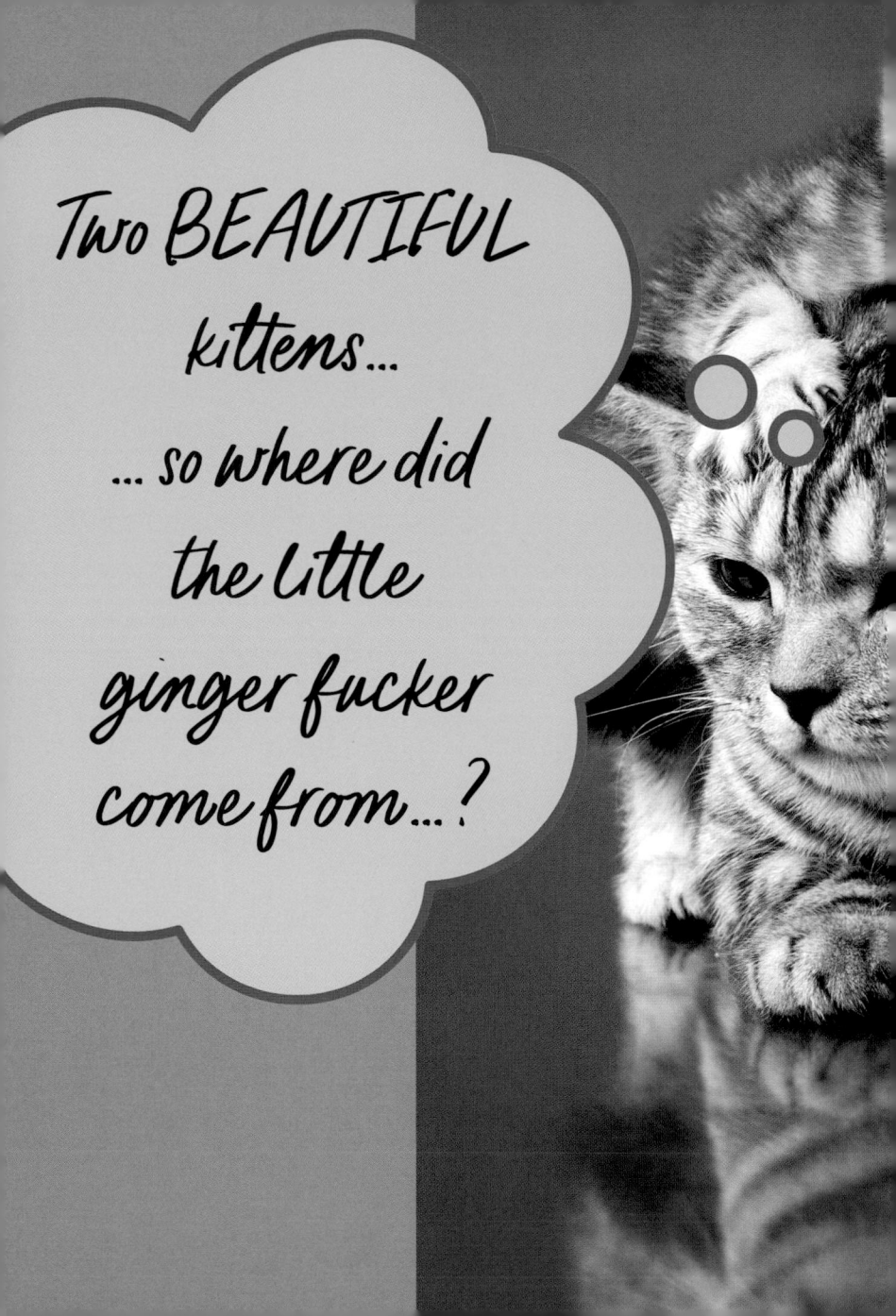
Two BEAUTIFUL kittens...
... so where did the little ginger fucker come from...?

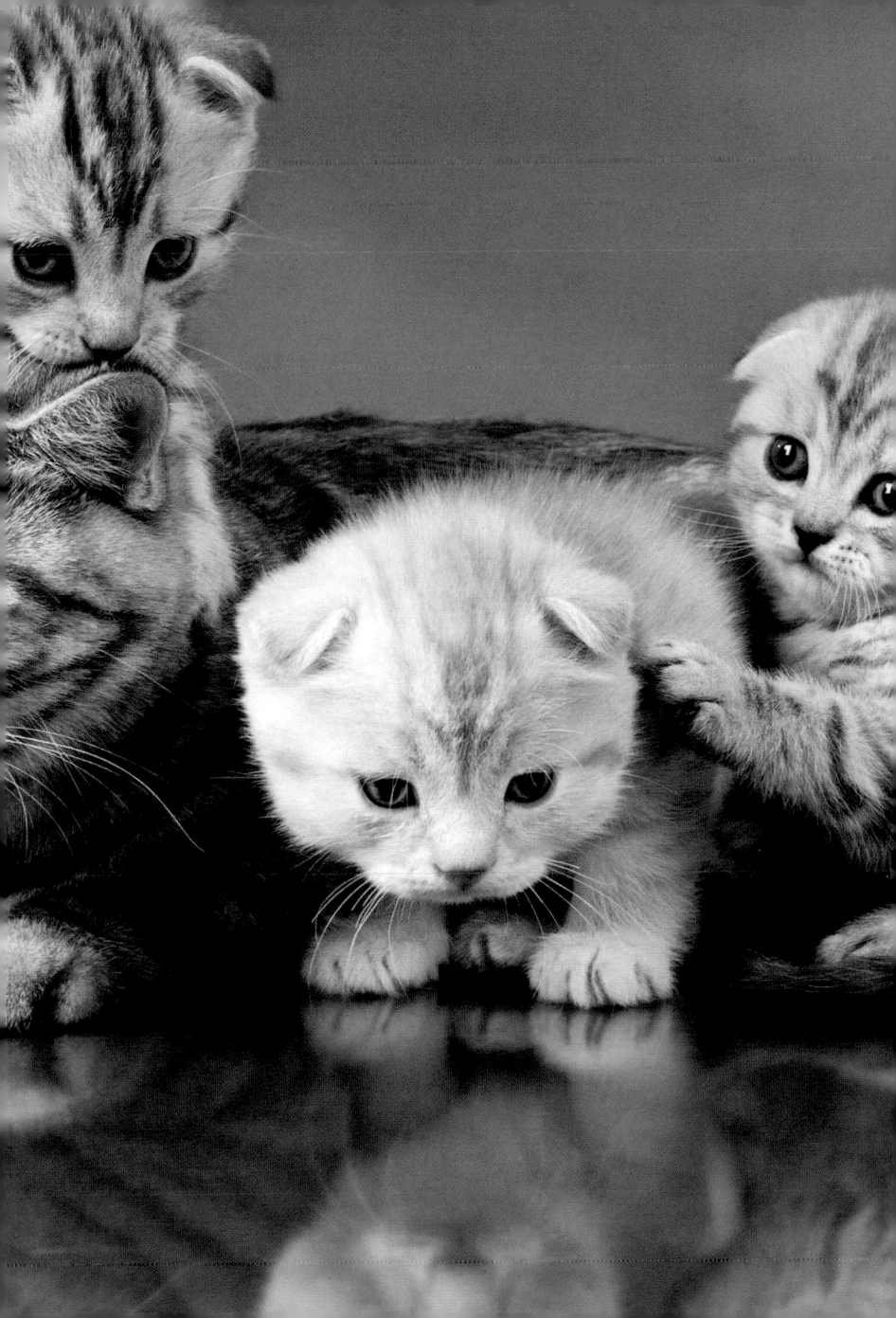

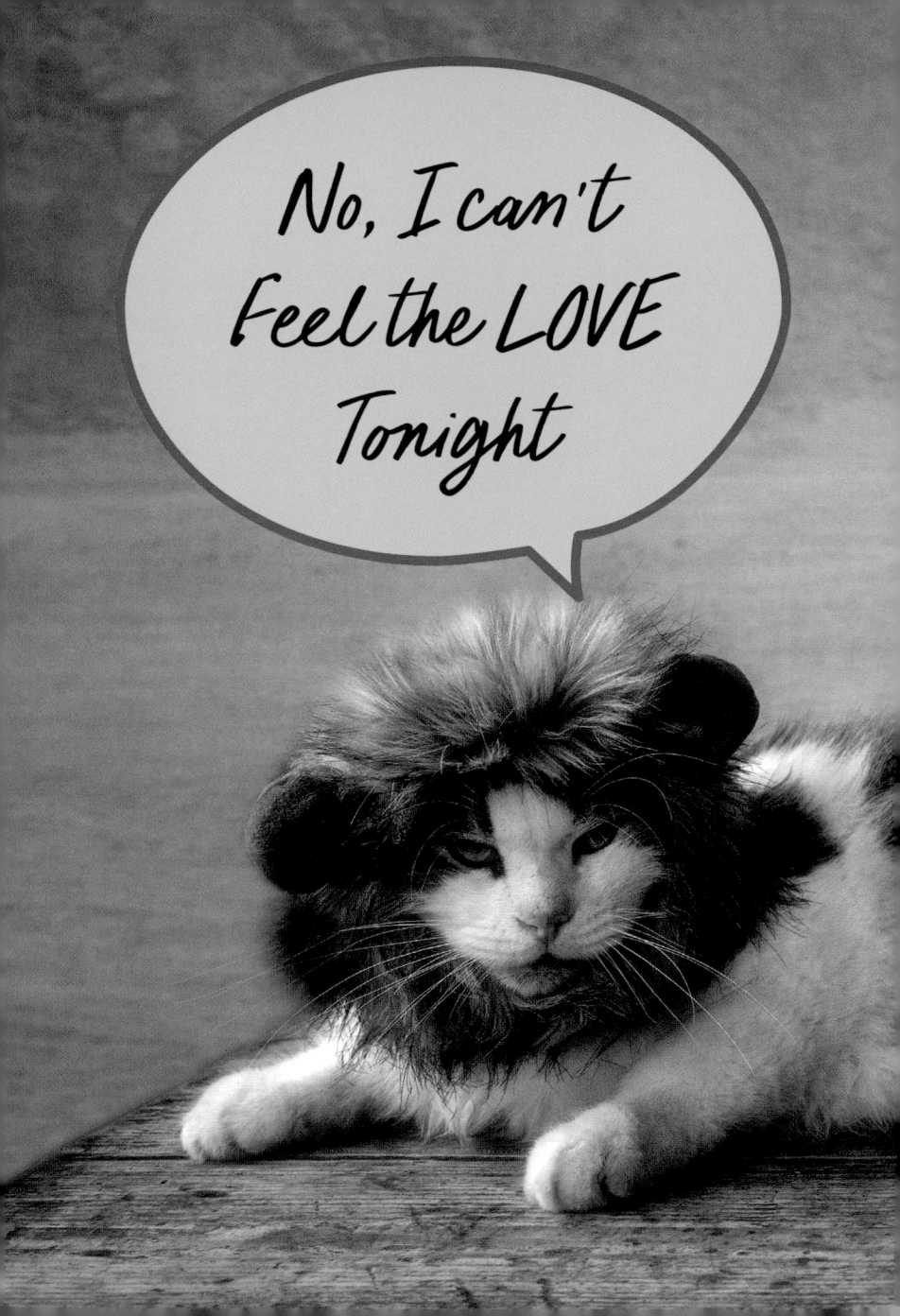
No, I can't
Feel the LOVE
Tonight

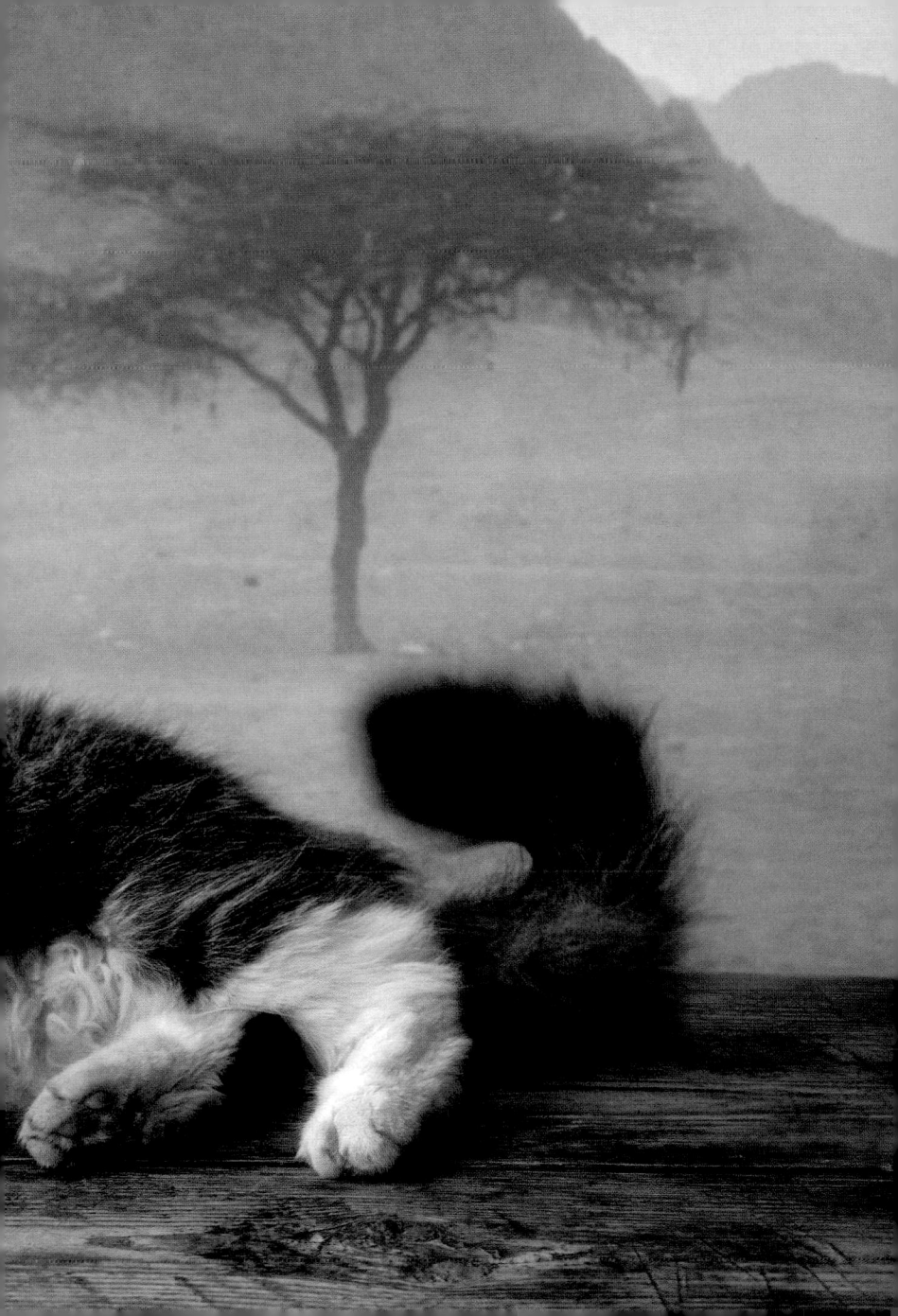

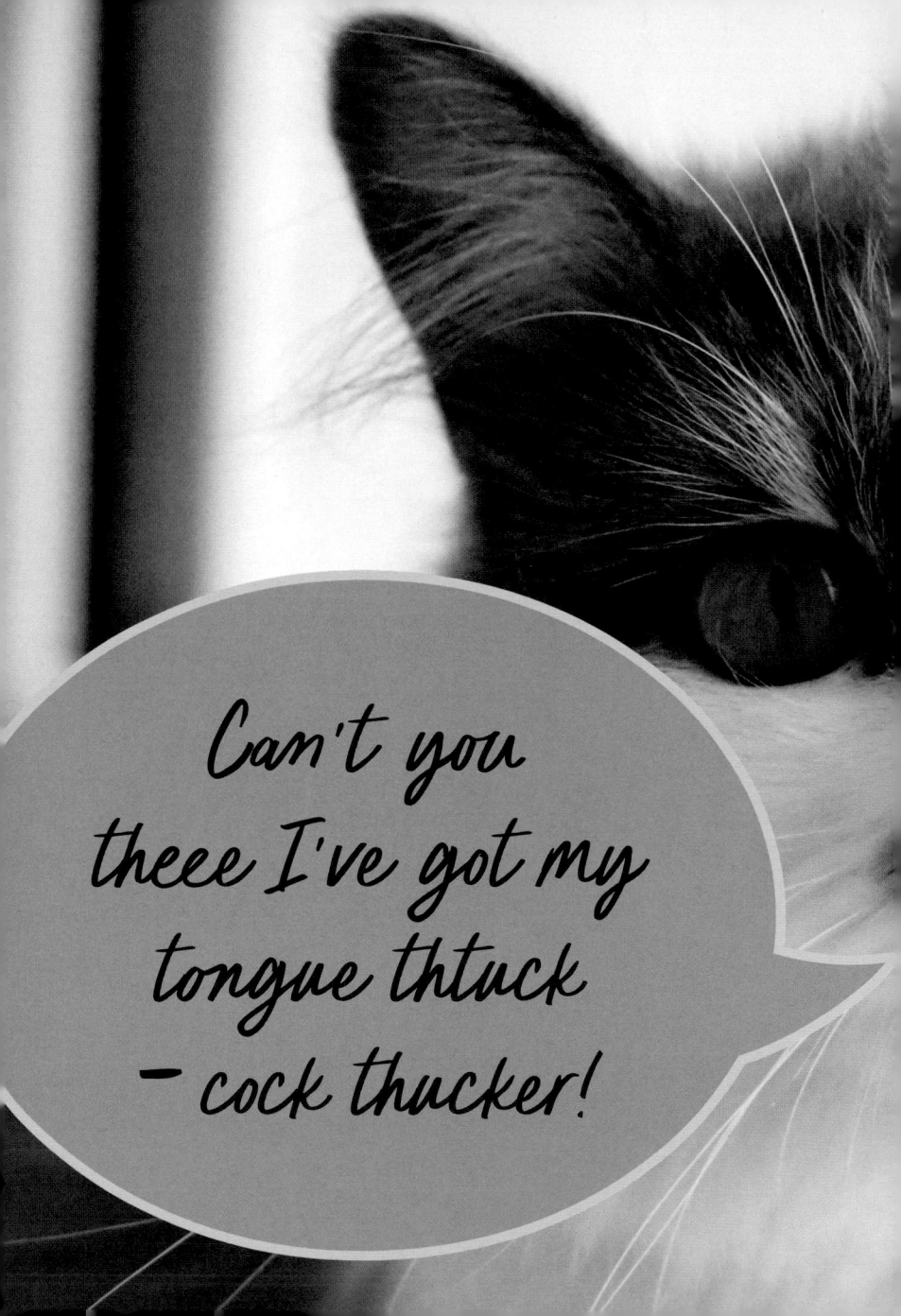
Can't you
theee I've got my
tongue thtuck
- cock thucker!

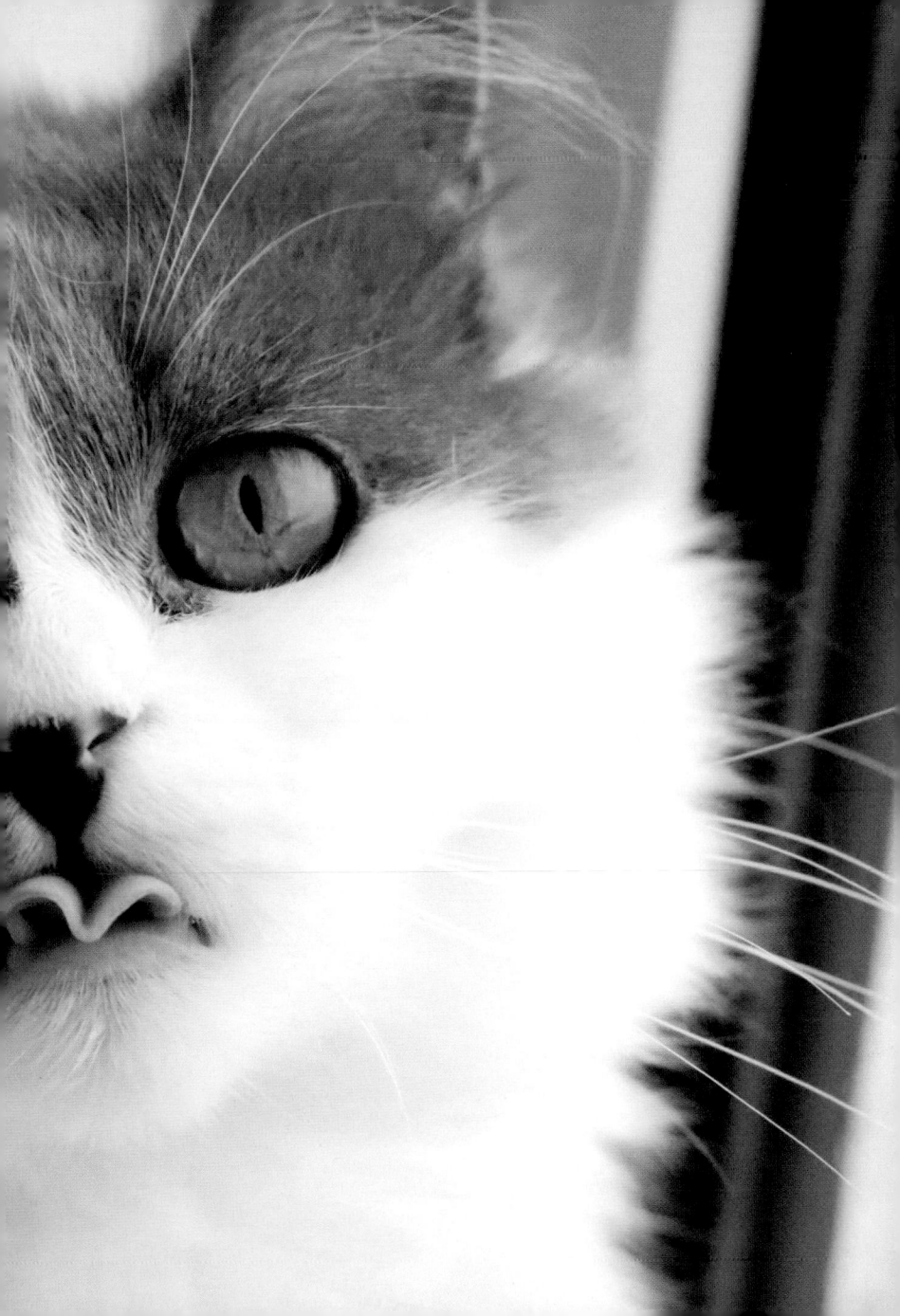

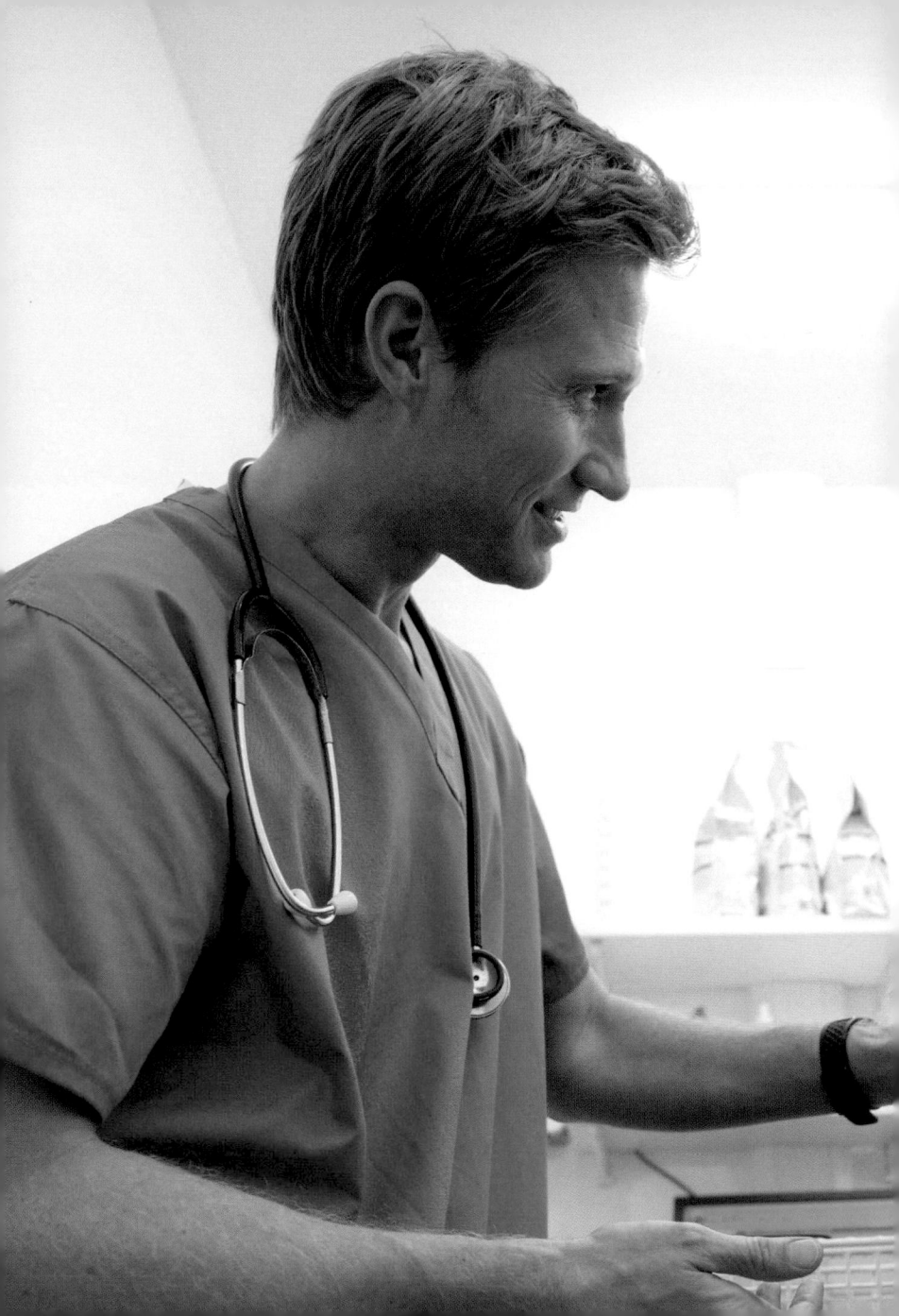

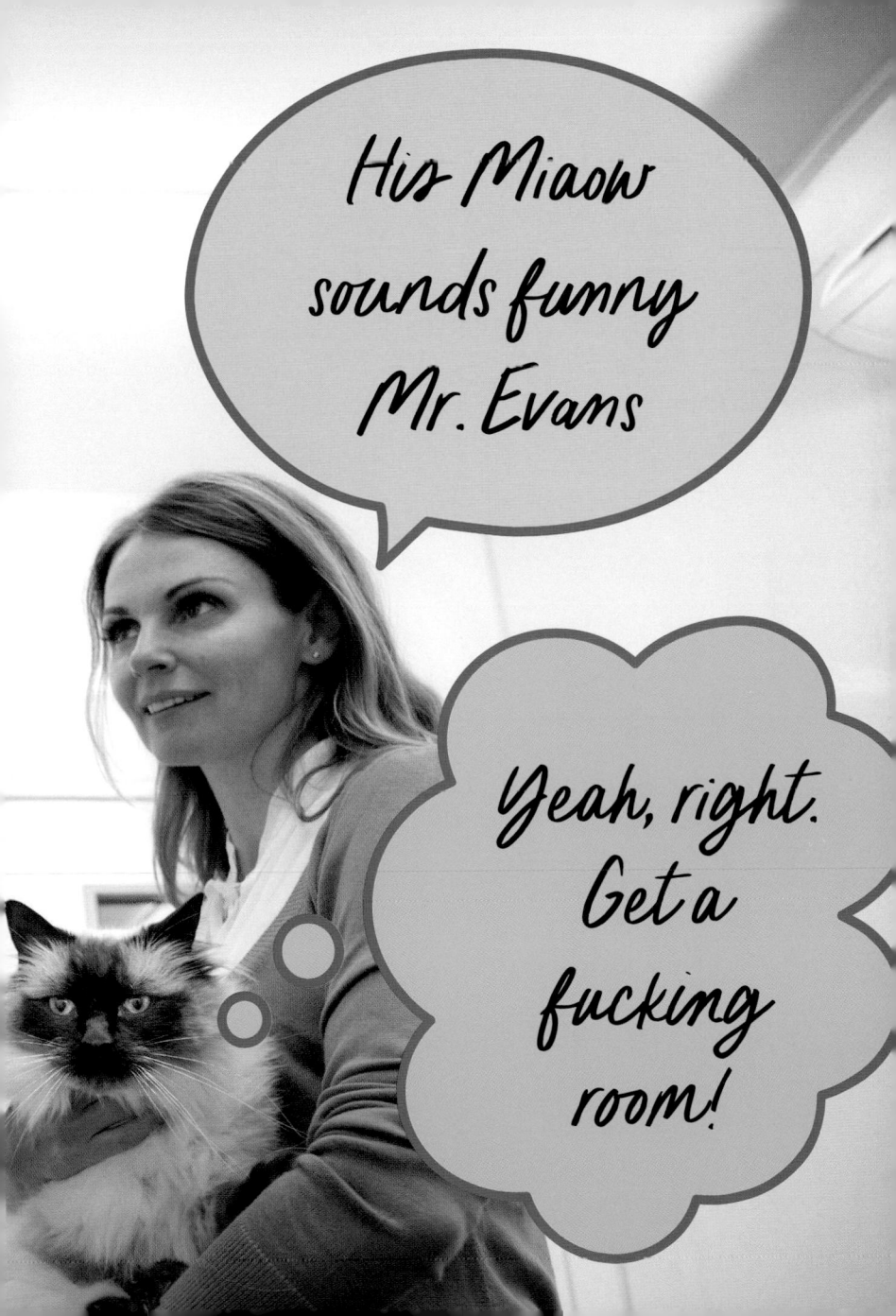
His Miaow sounds funny Mr. Evans
Yeah, right. Get a fucking room!

Yes, I AM
silently judging you.
Hipster twat

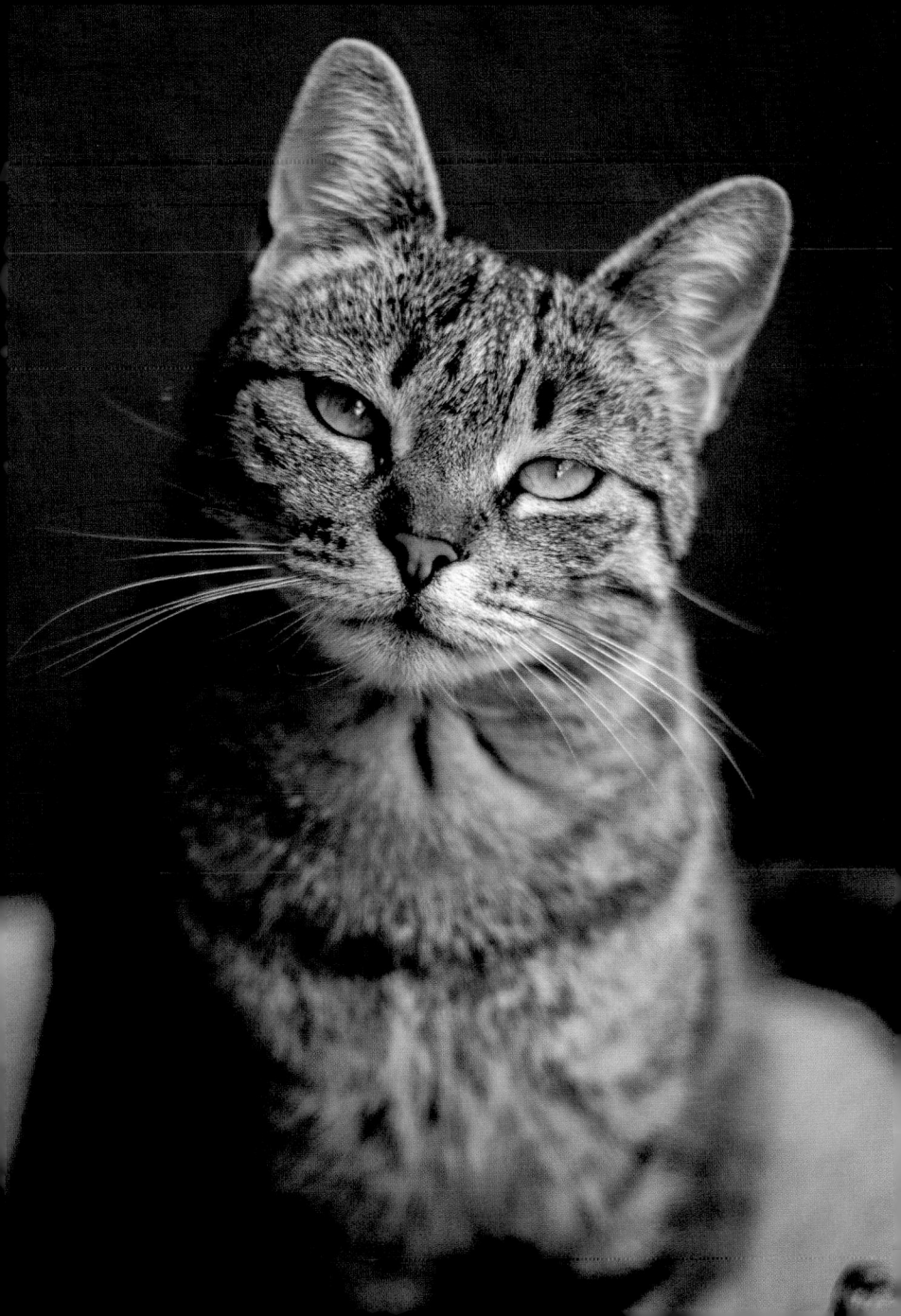

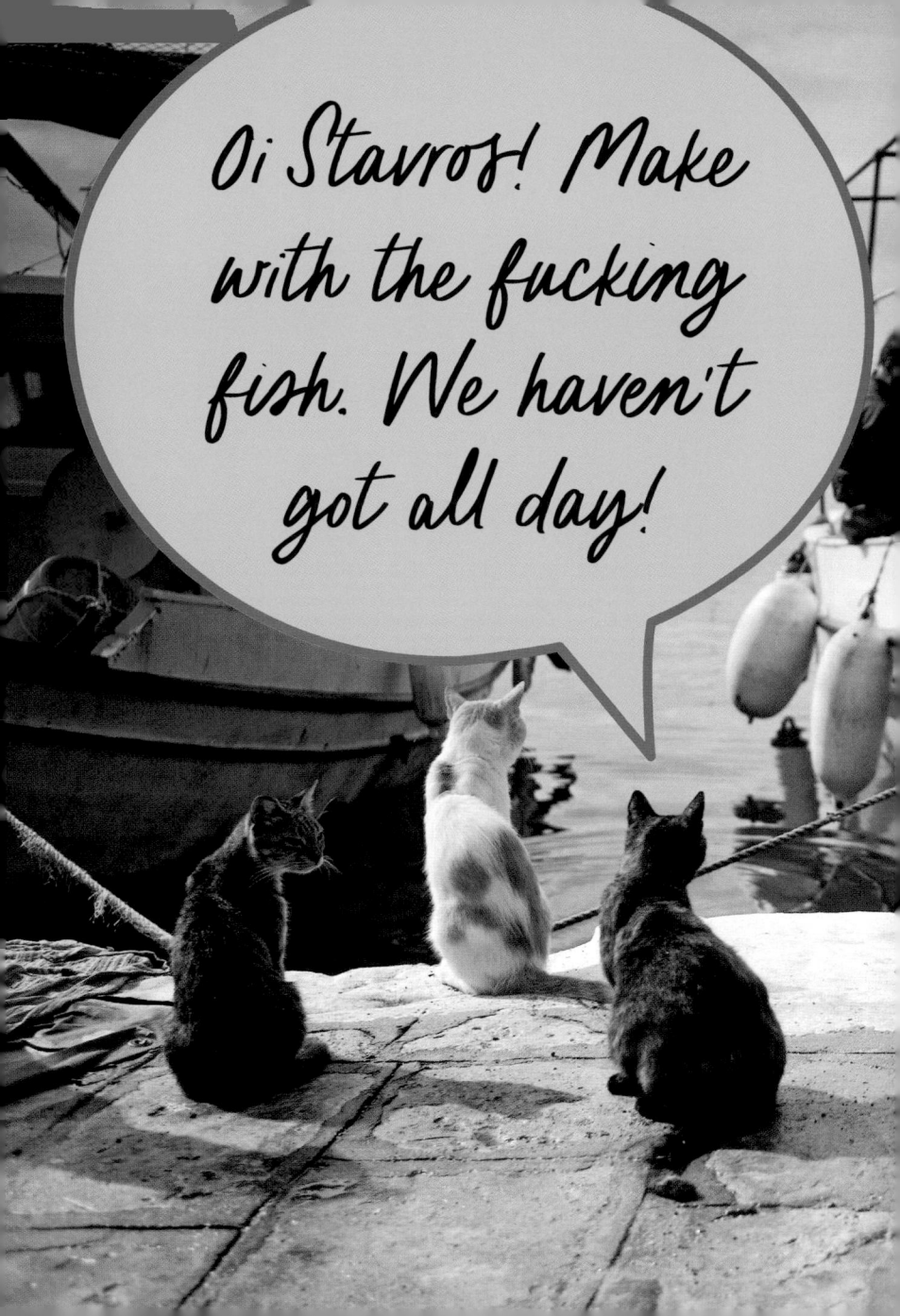
Oi Stavros! Make with the fucking fish. We haven't got all day!

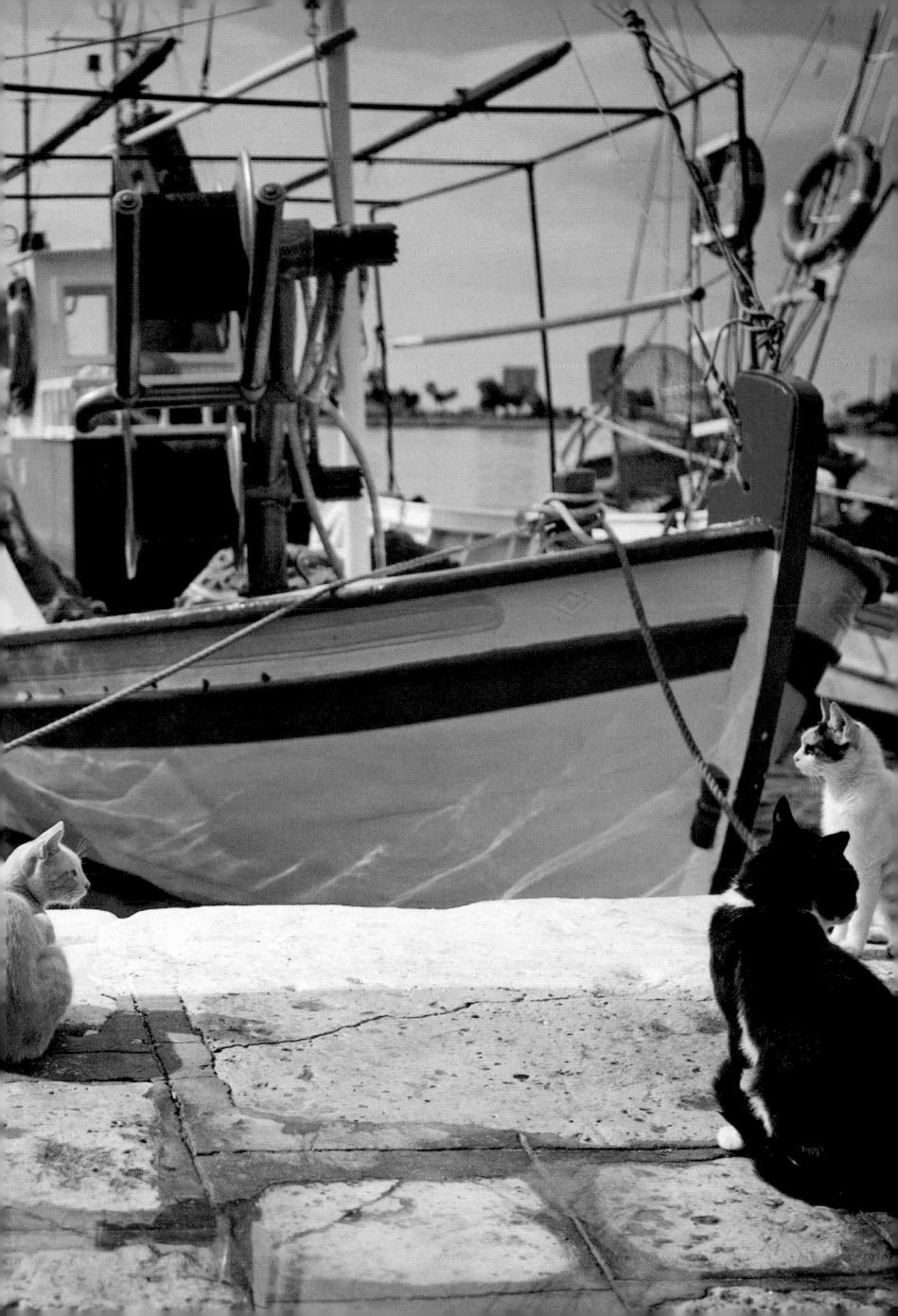

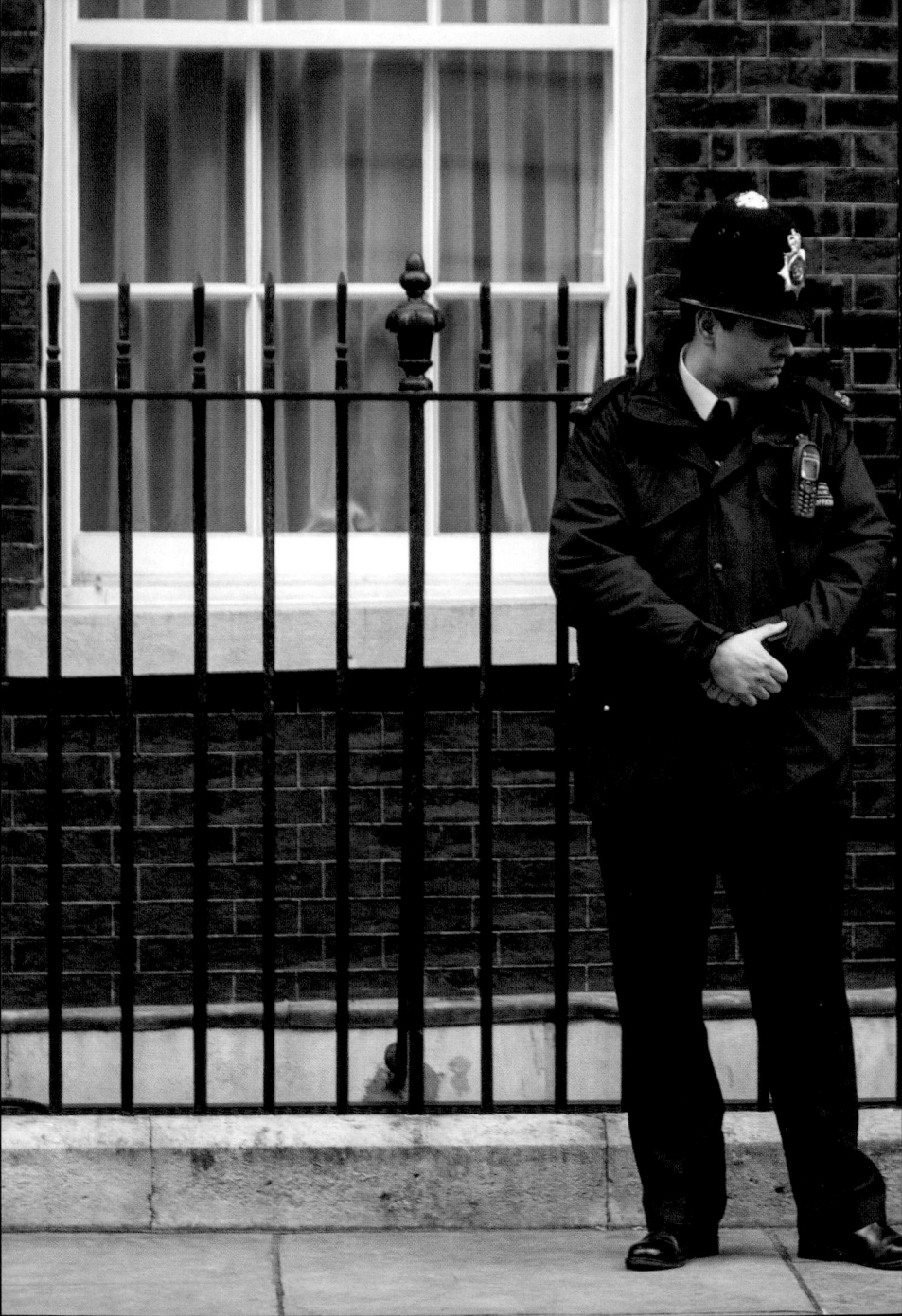

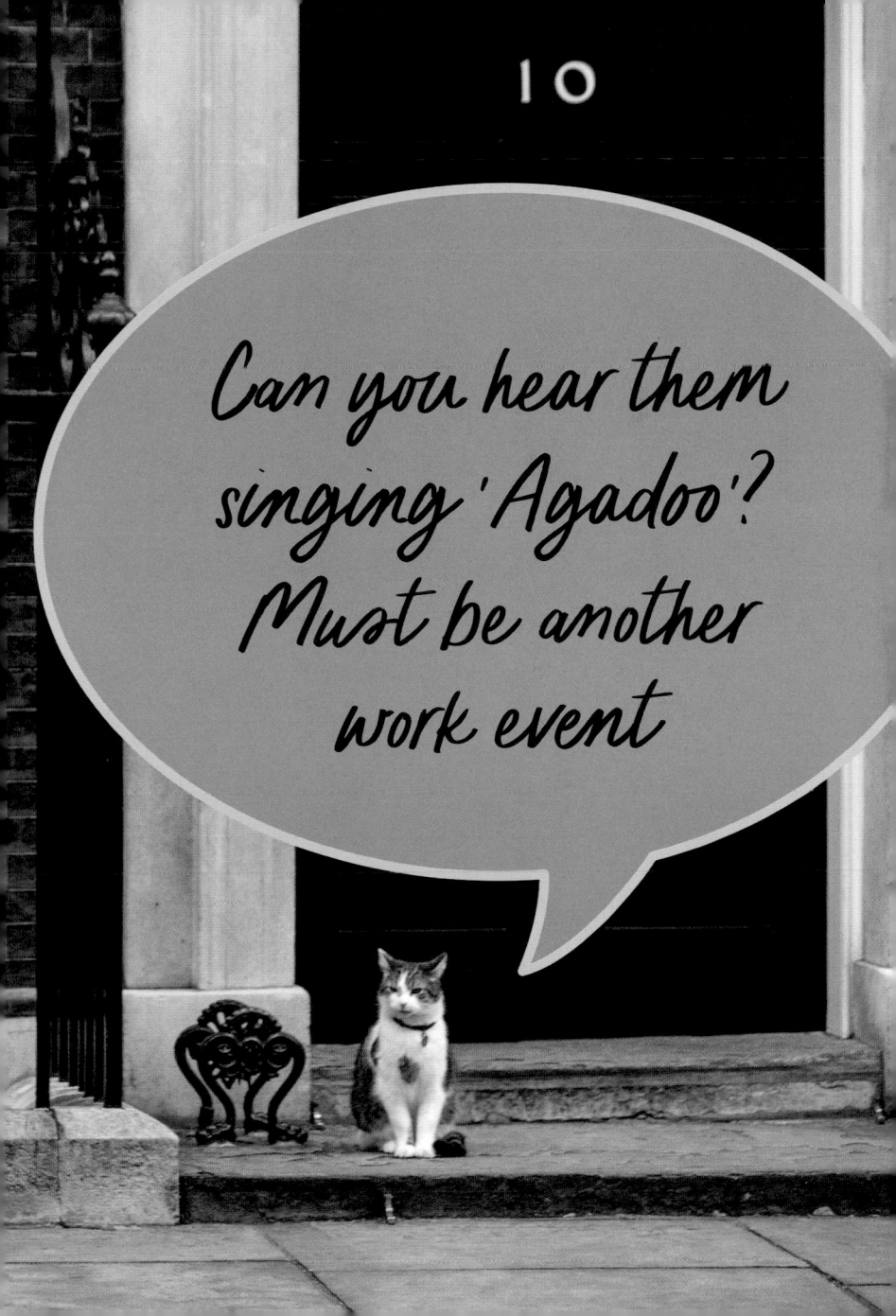
10
Can you hear them singing 'Agadoo'? Must be another work event

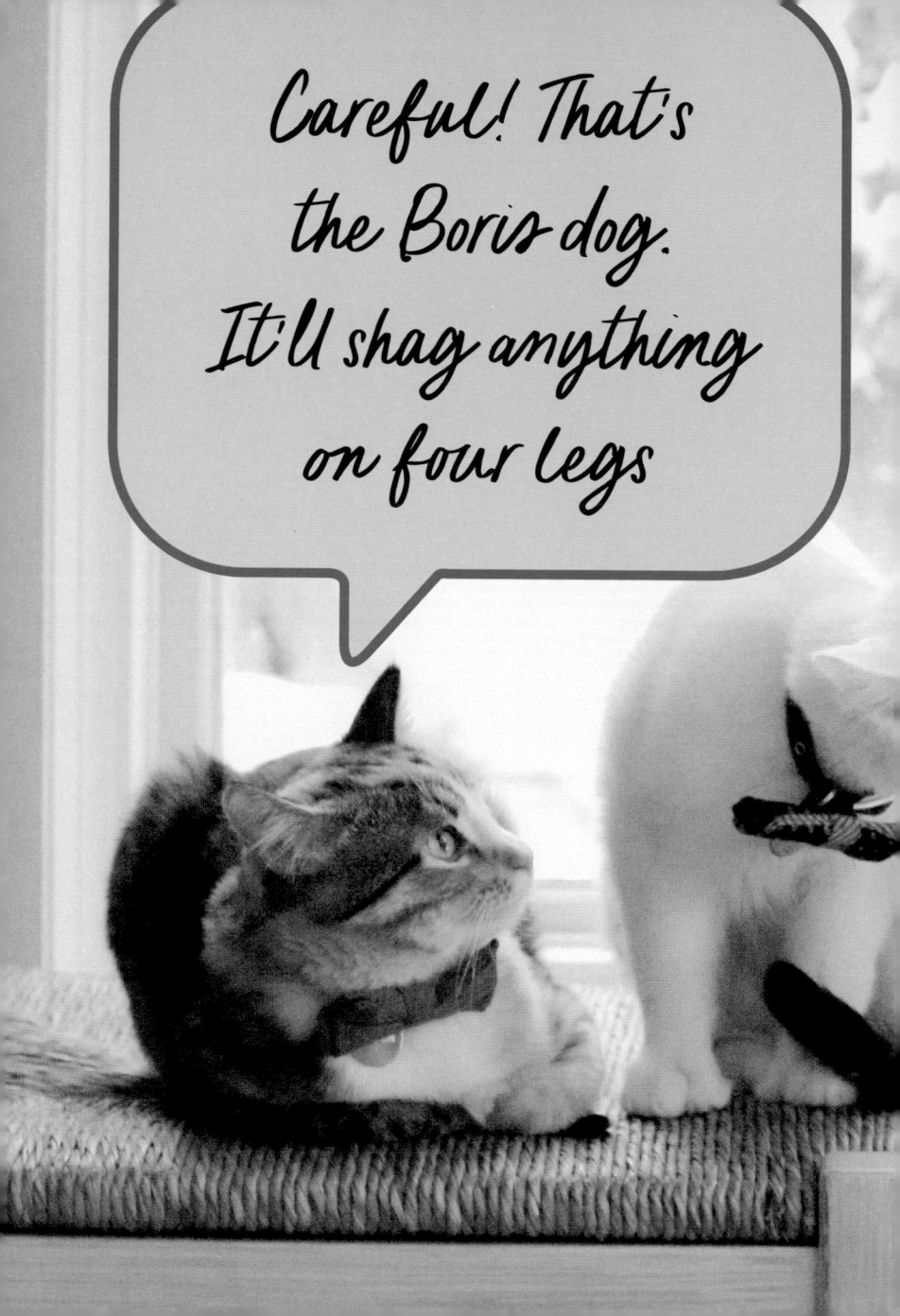
Careful! That's the Boris dog. It'll shag anything on four legs

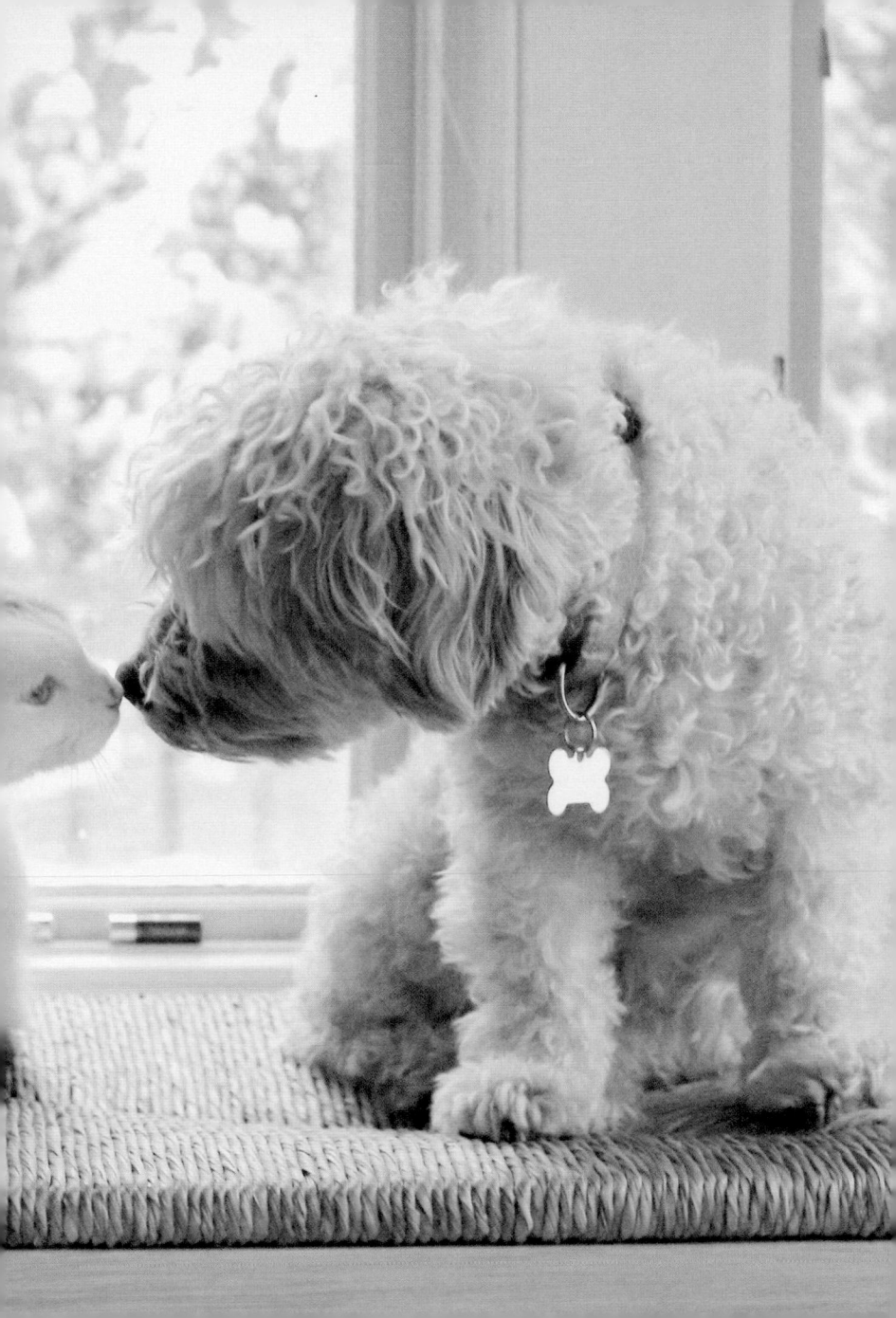

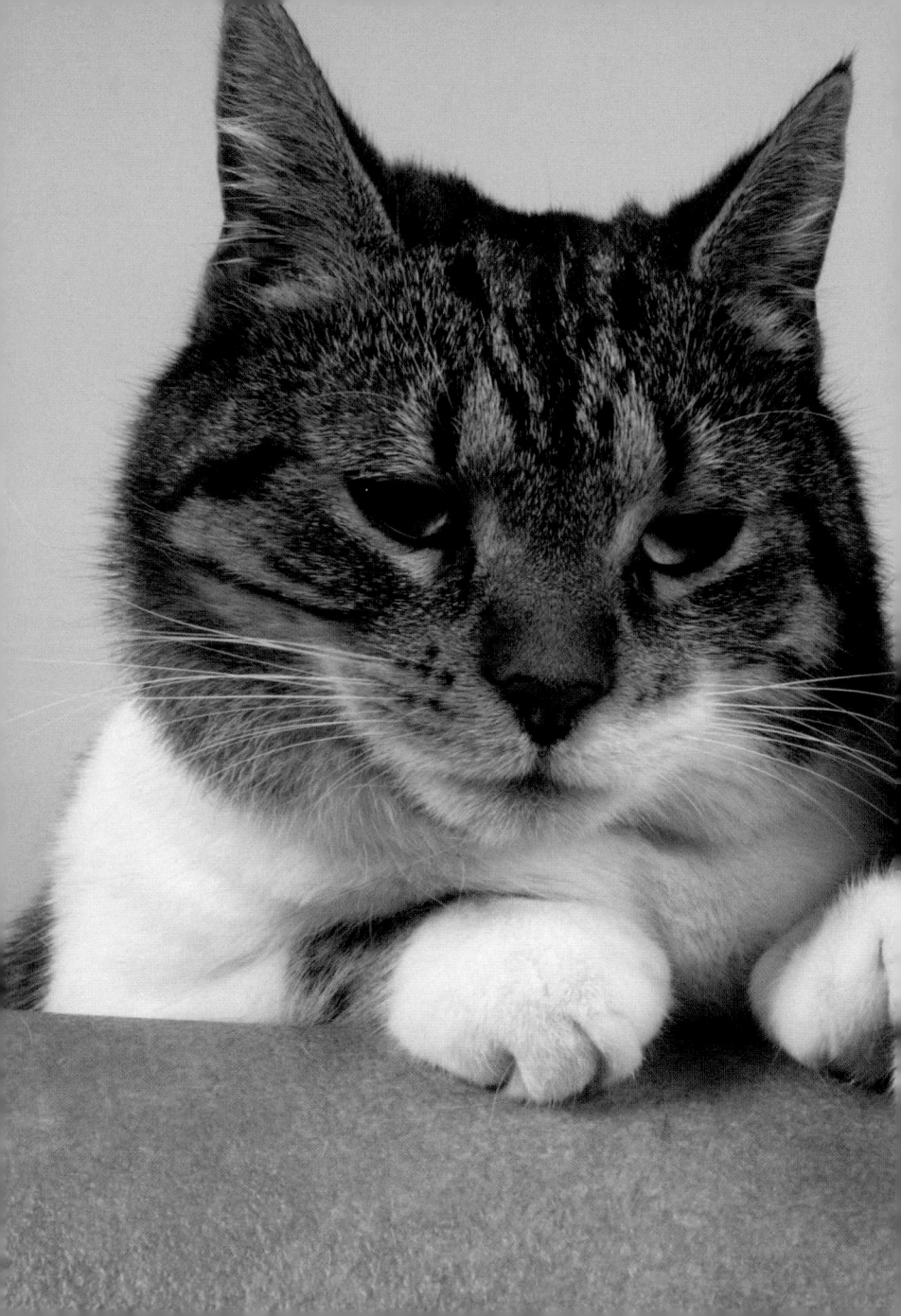

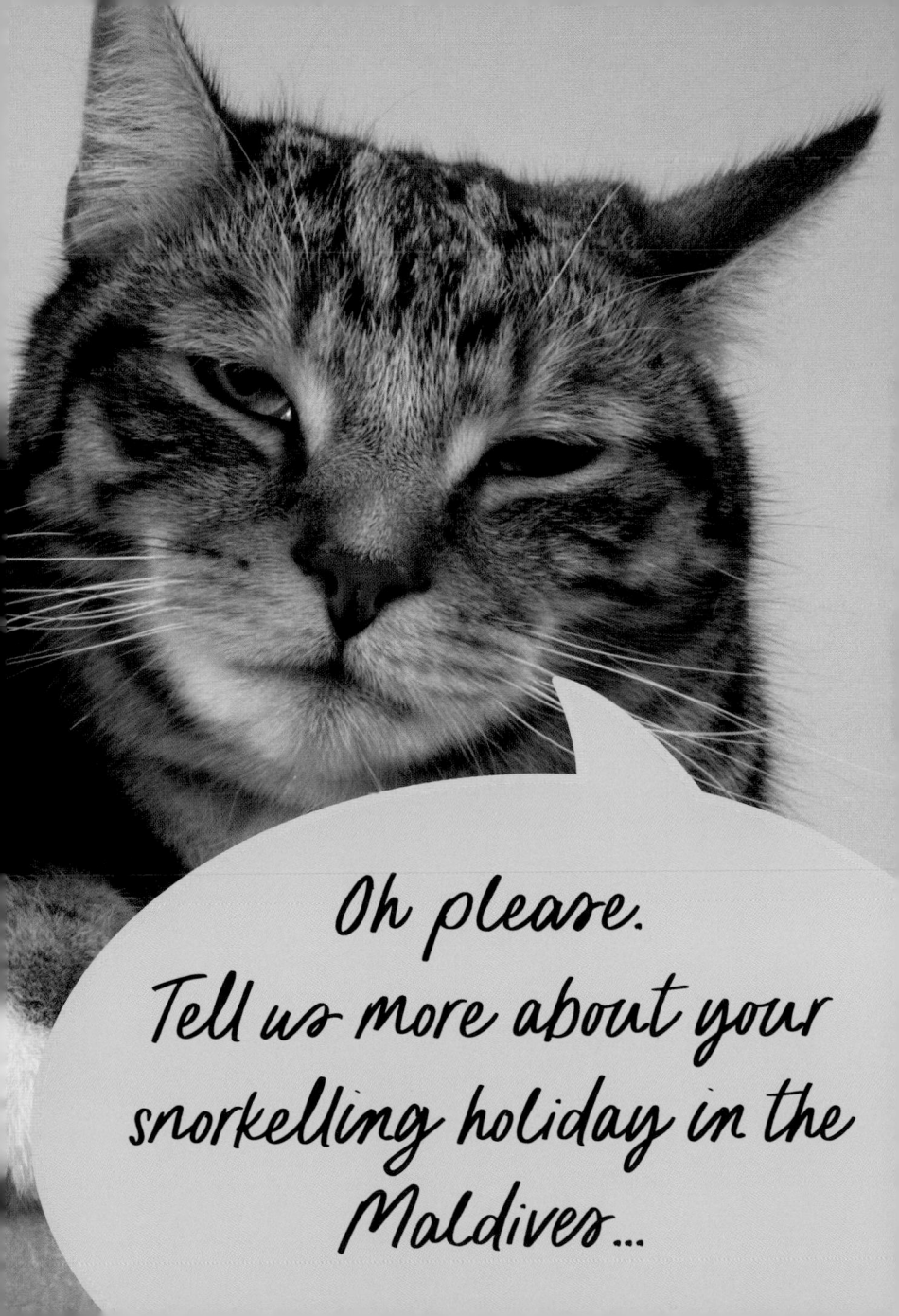
Oh please.
Tell us more about your
snorkelling holiday in the
Maldives...

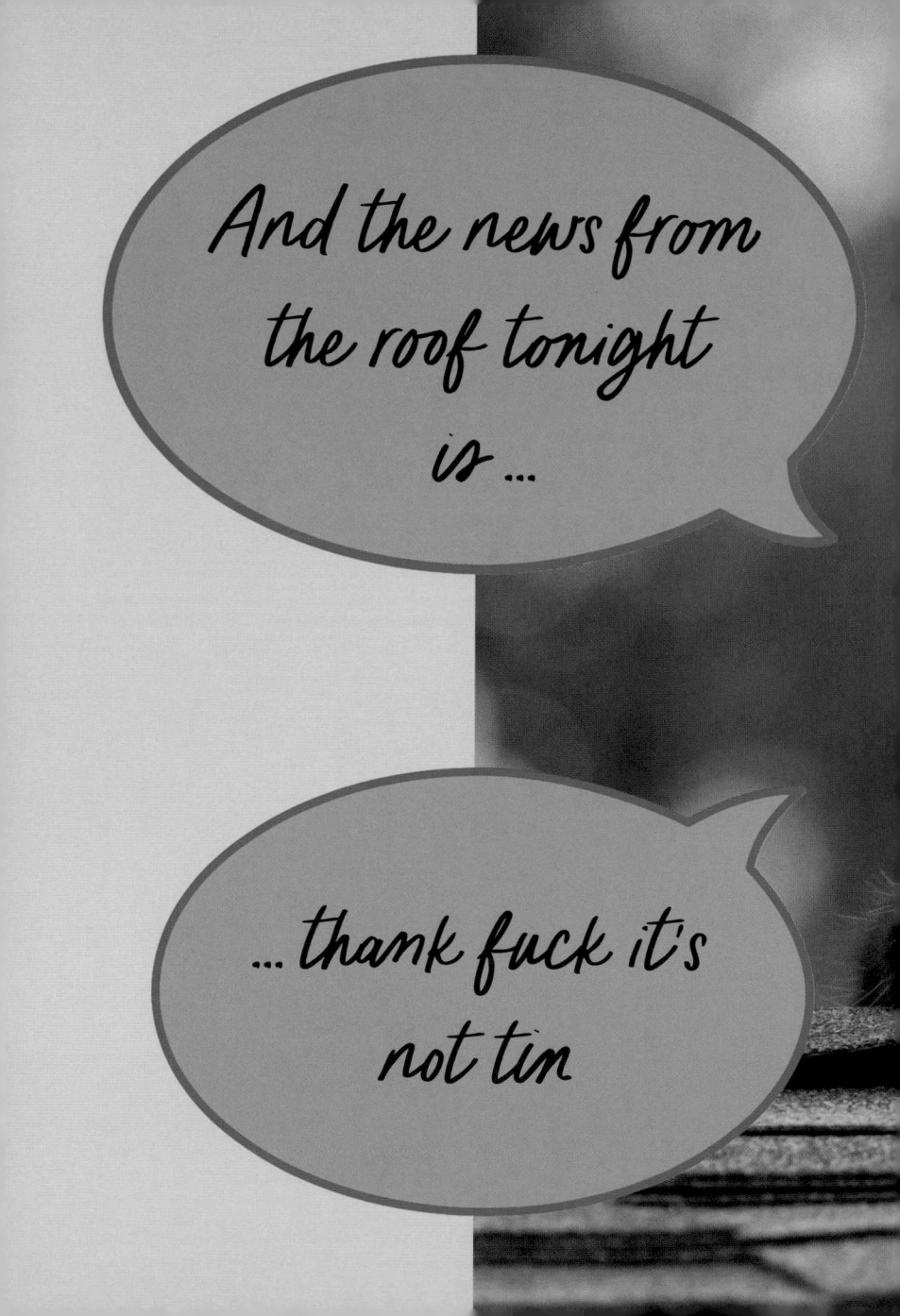
And the news from the roof tonight is ...
... thank fuck it's not tin

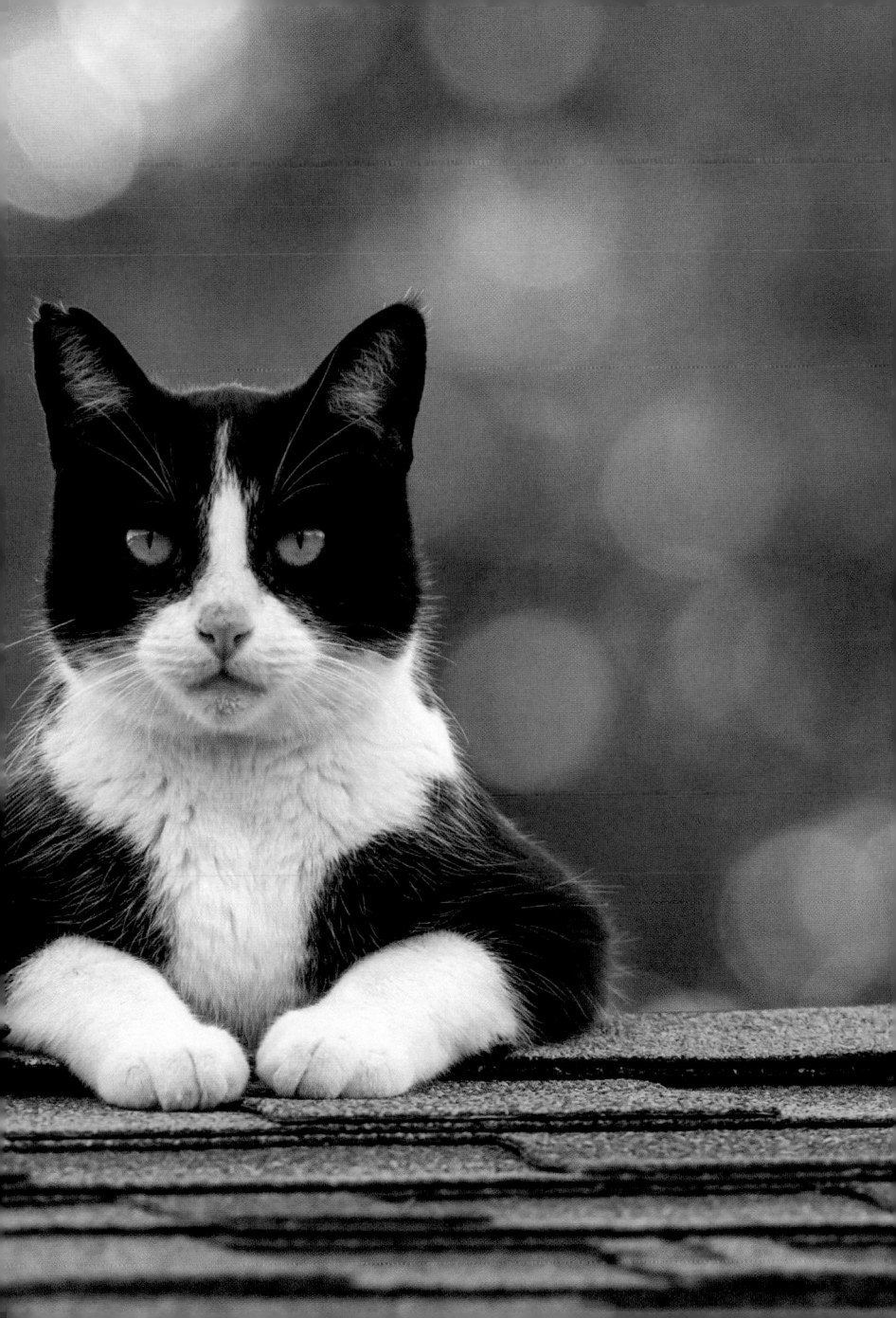

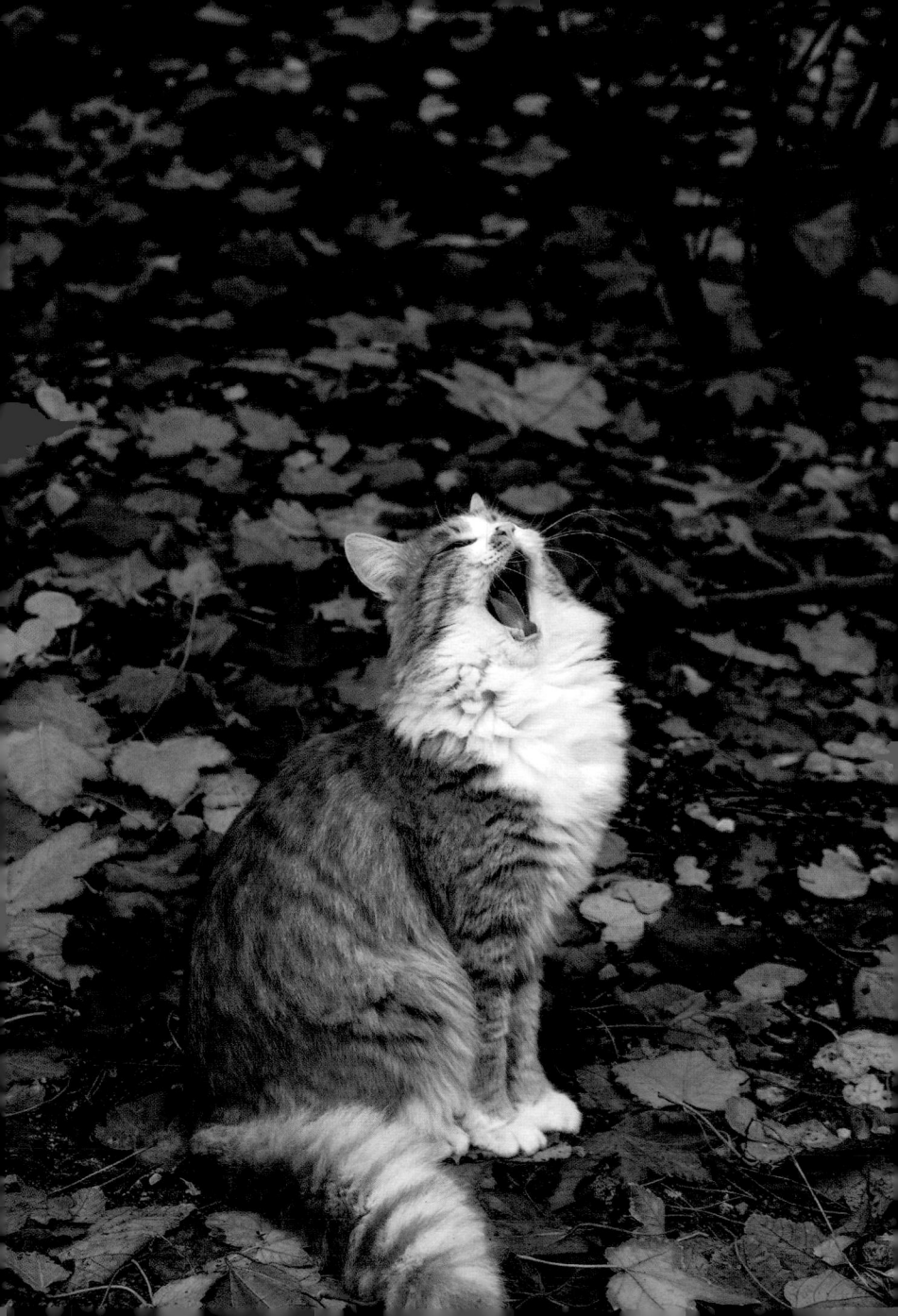

Fuck me ...
outside's boring

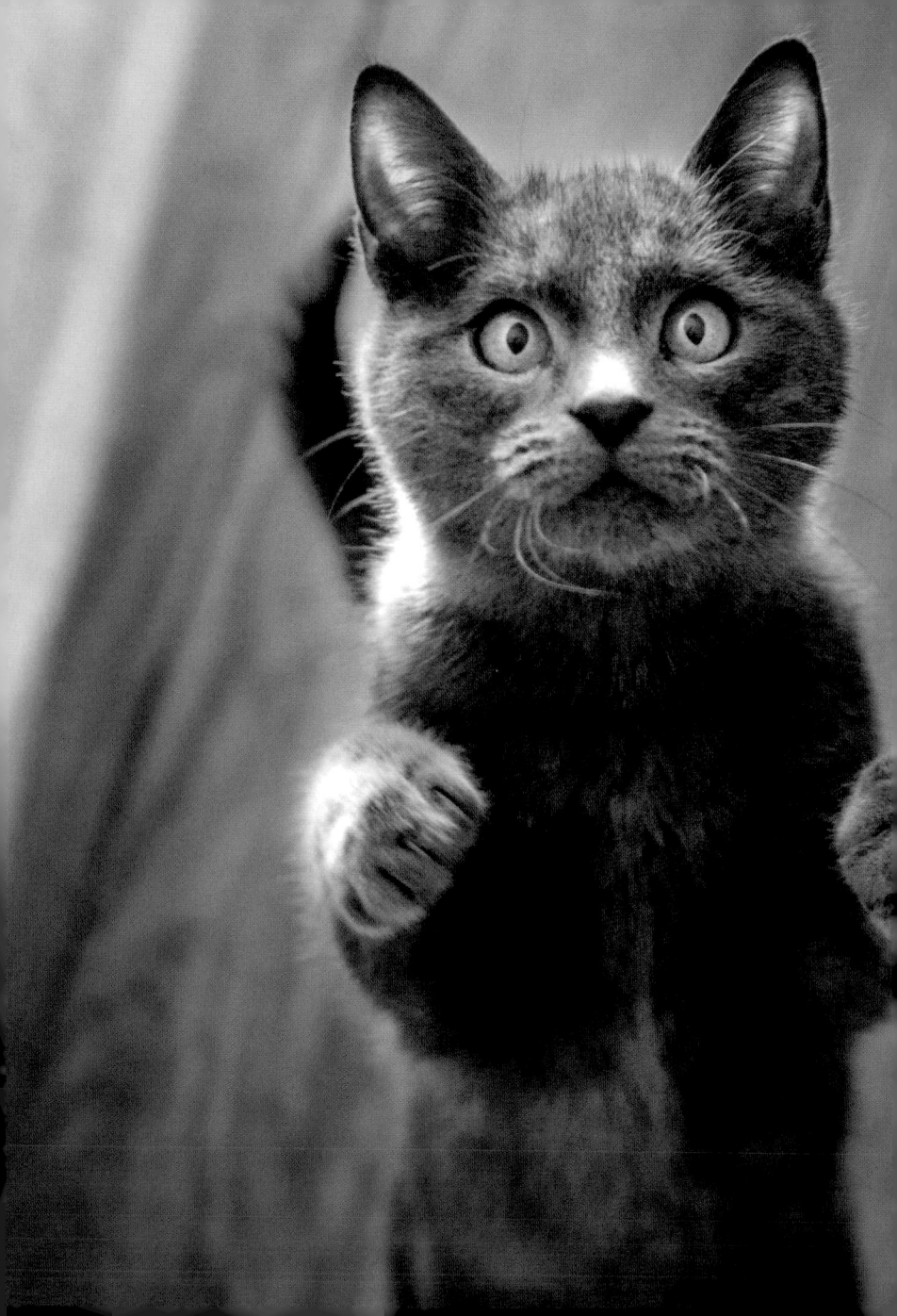

Um, remember me...? I'm the pet you haven't fed for a day thanks to your three bottles of Prosecco on Friday night.

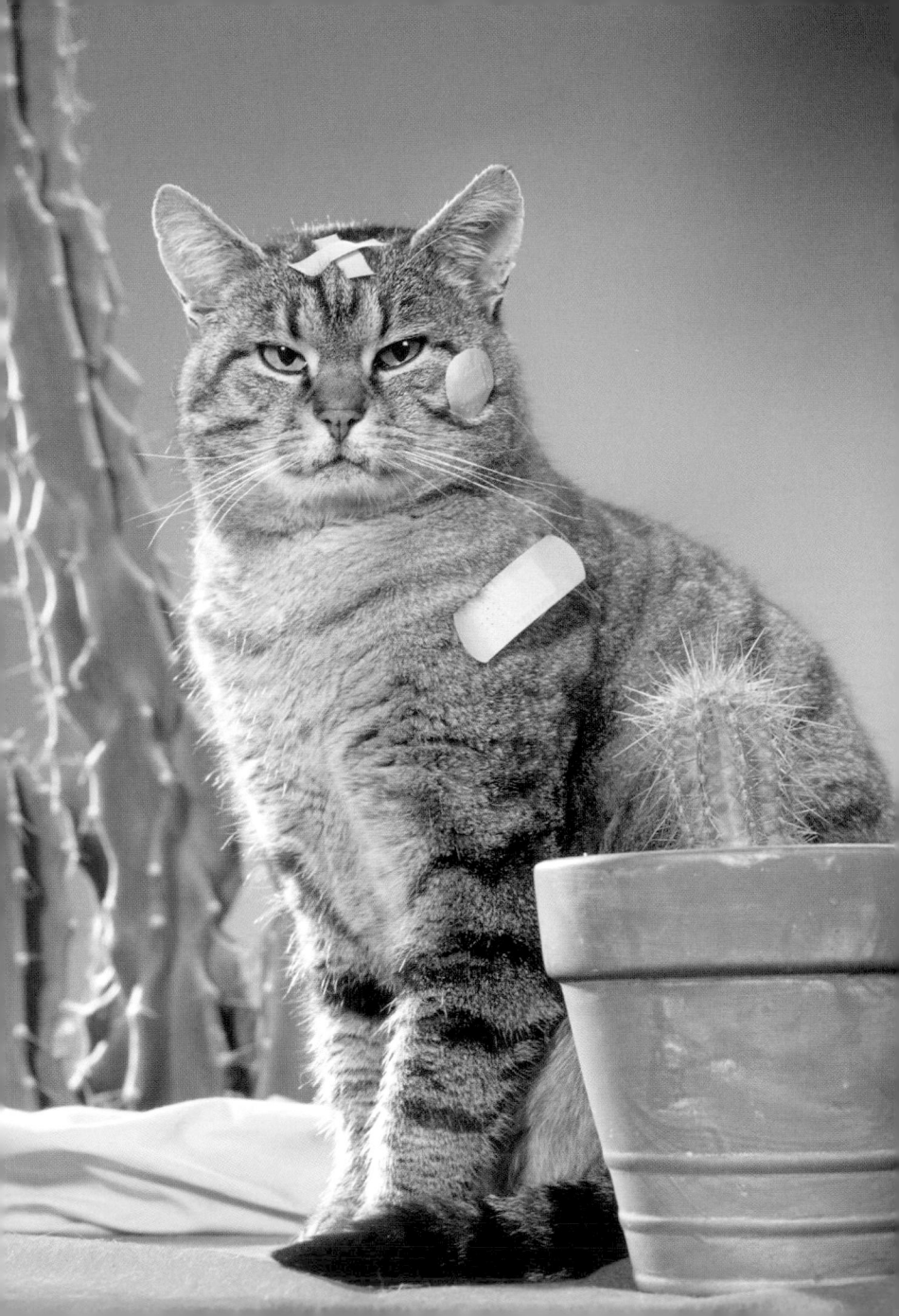

I can't believe that wanker bought a cactus. I clearly said, "Catmint!"

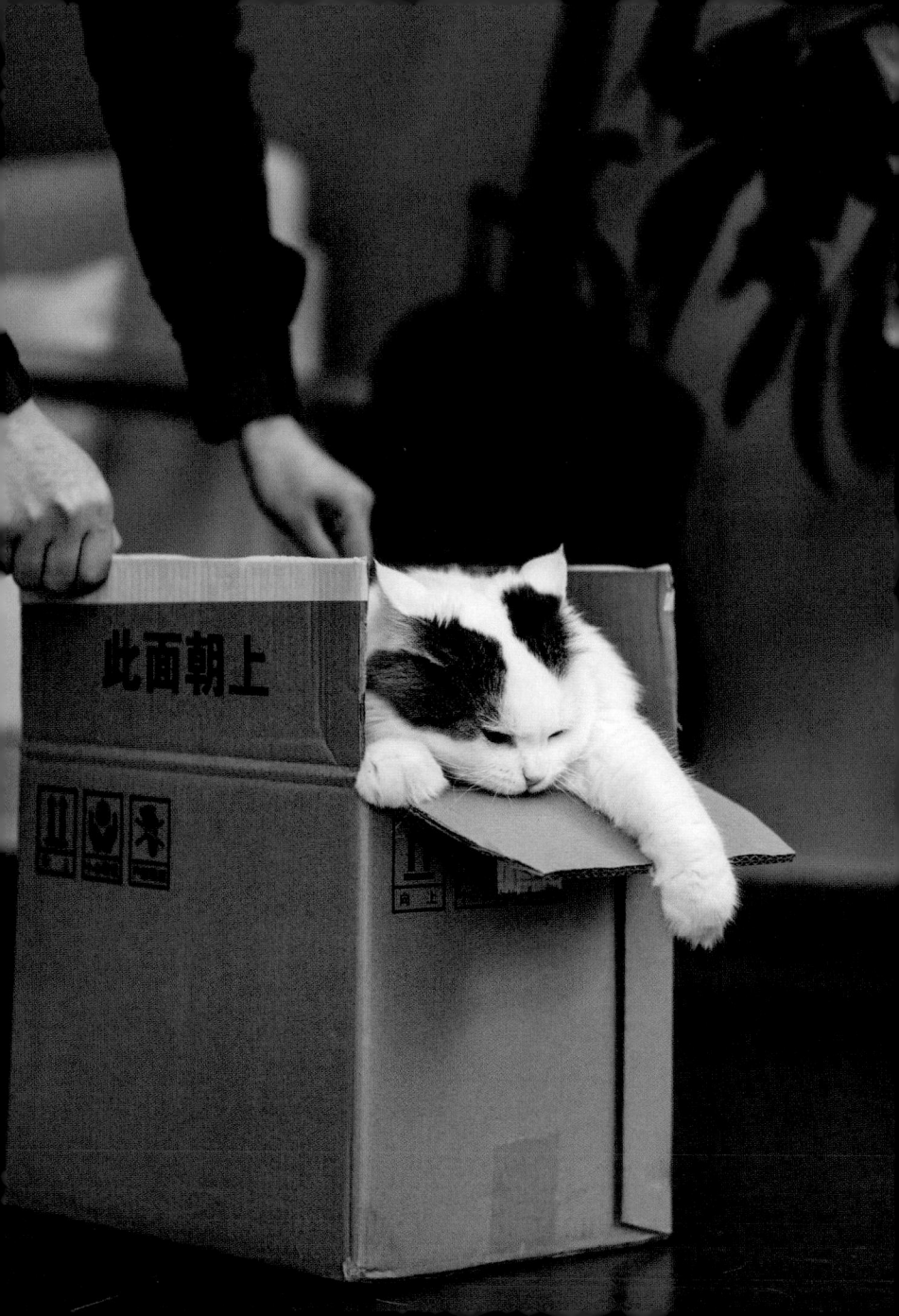
此面朝上

They're
NOT mailing me to
the cattery again!

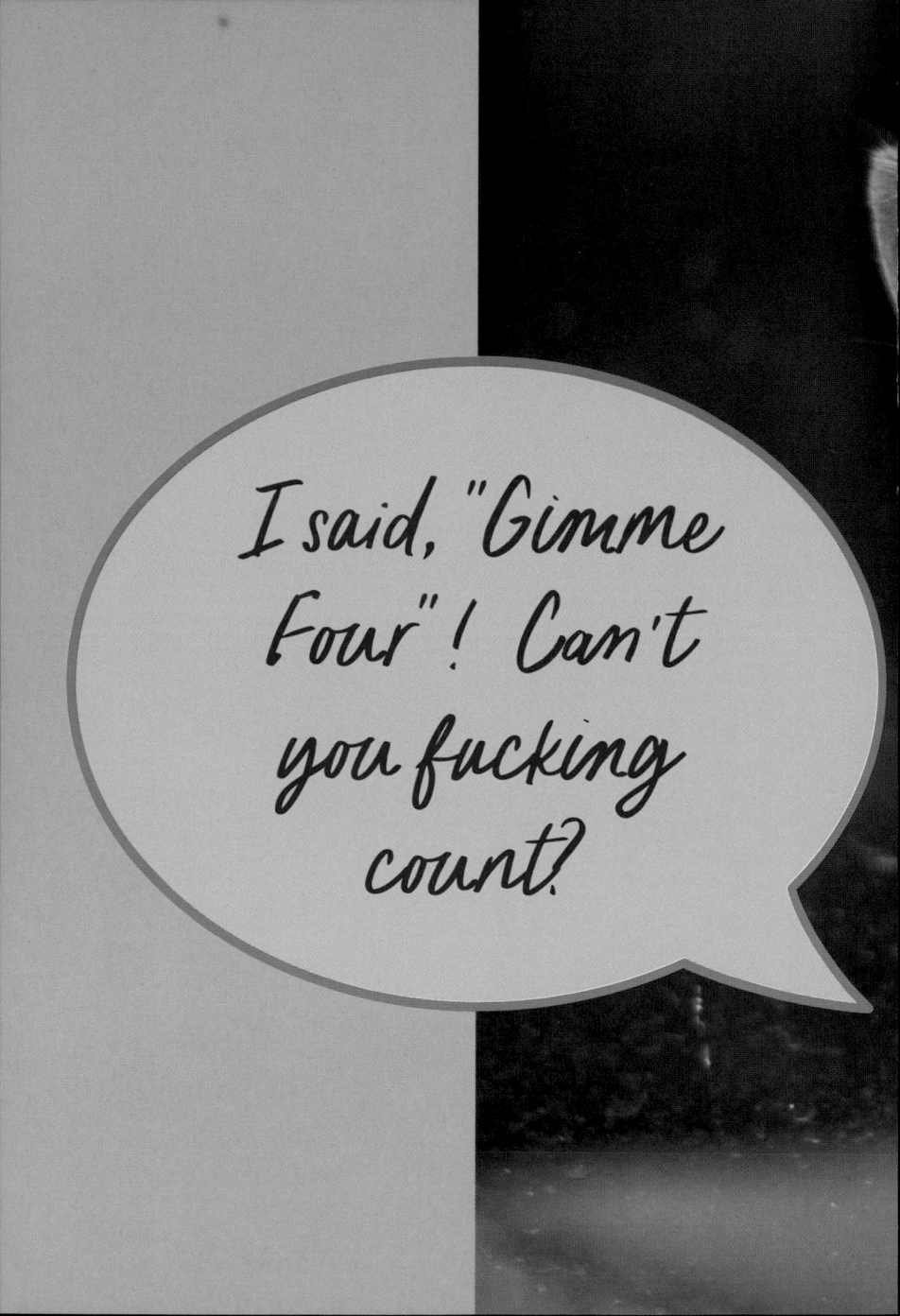
I said, "Gimme Four"! Can't you fucking count?

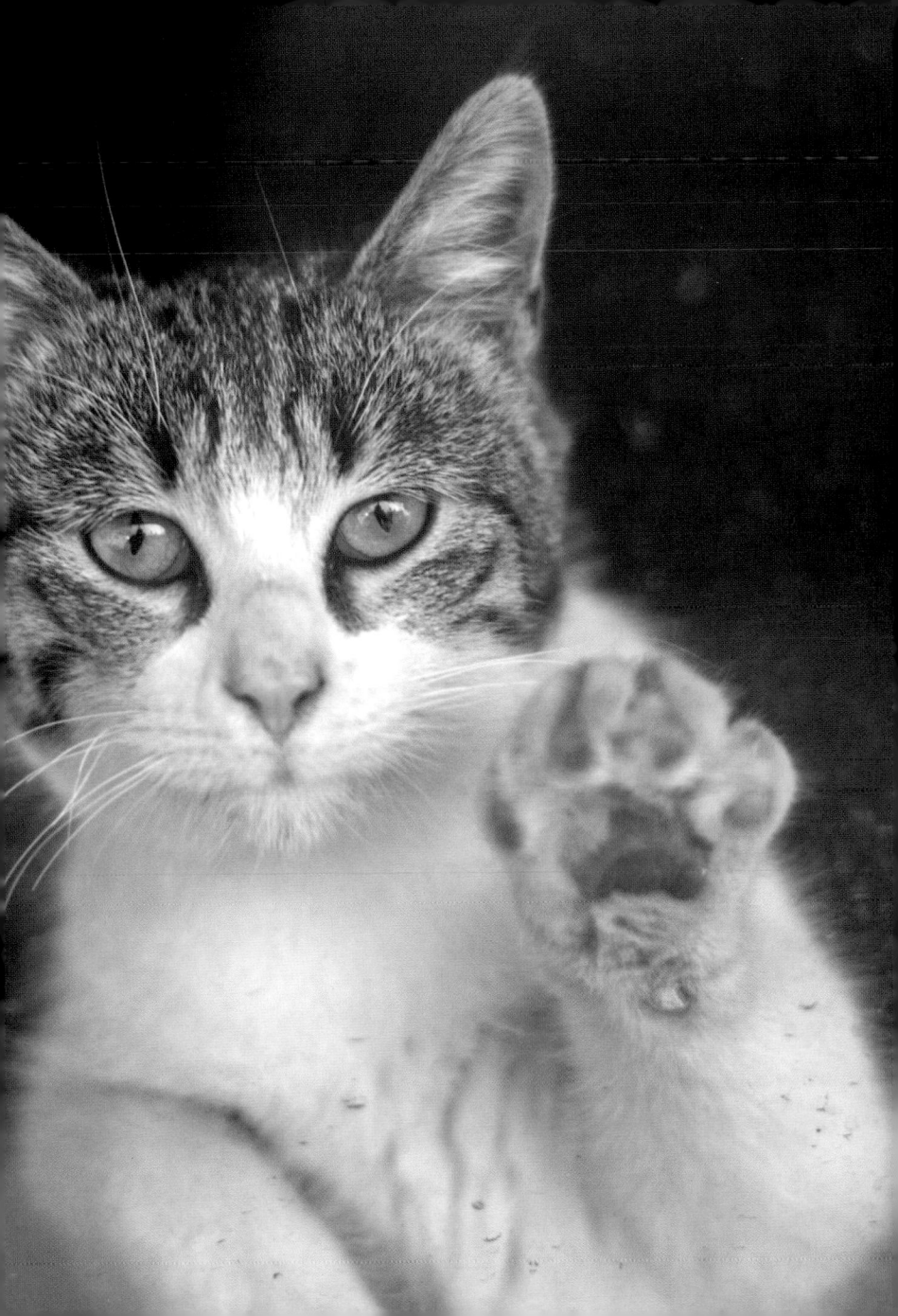

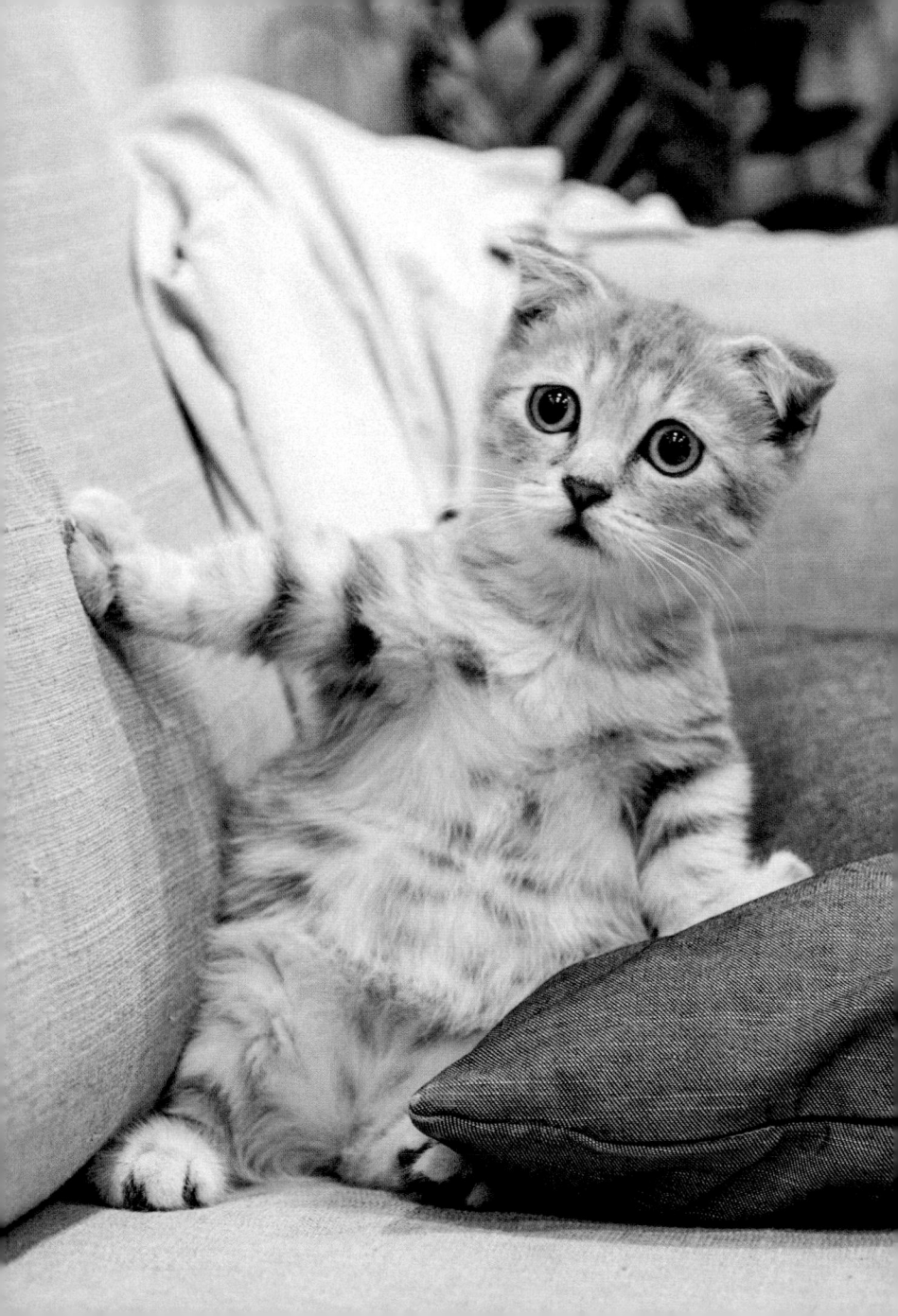

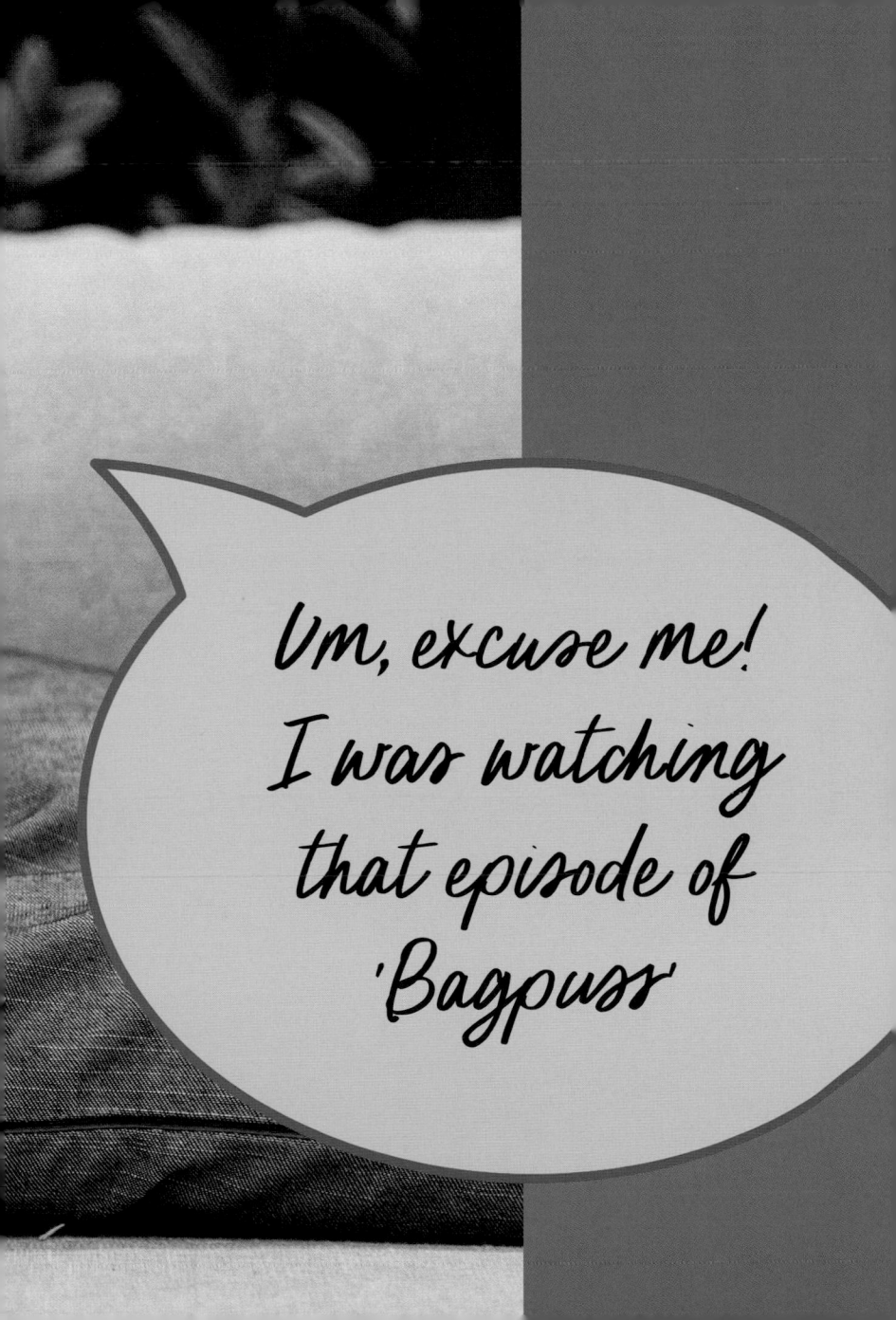
Um, excuse me!
I was watching
that episode of
'Bagpuss'

Yeah, right, do I look like a fucking peony...?

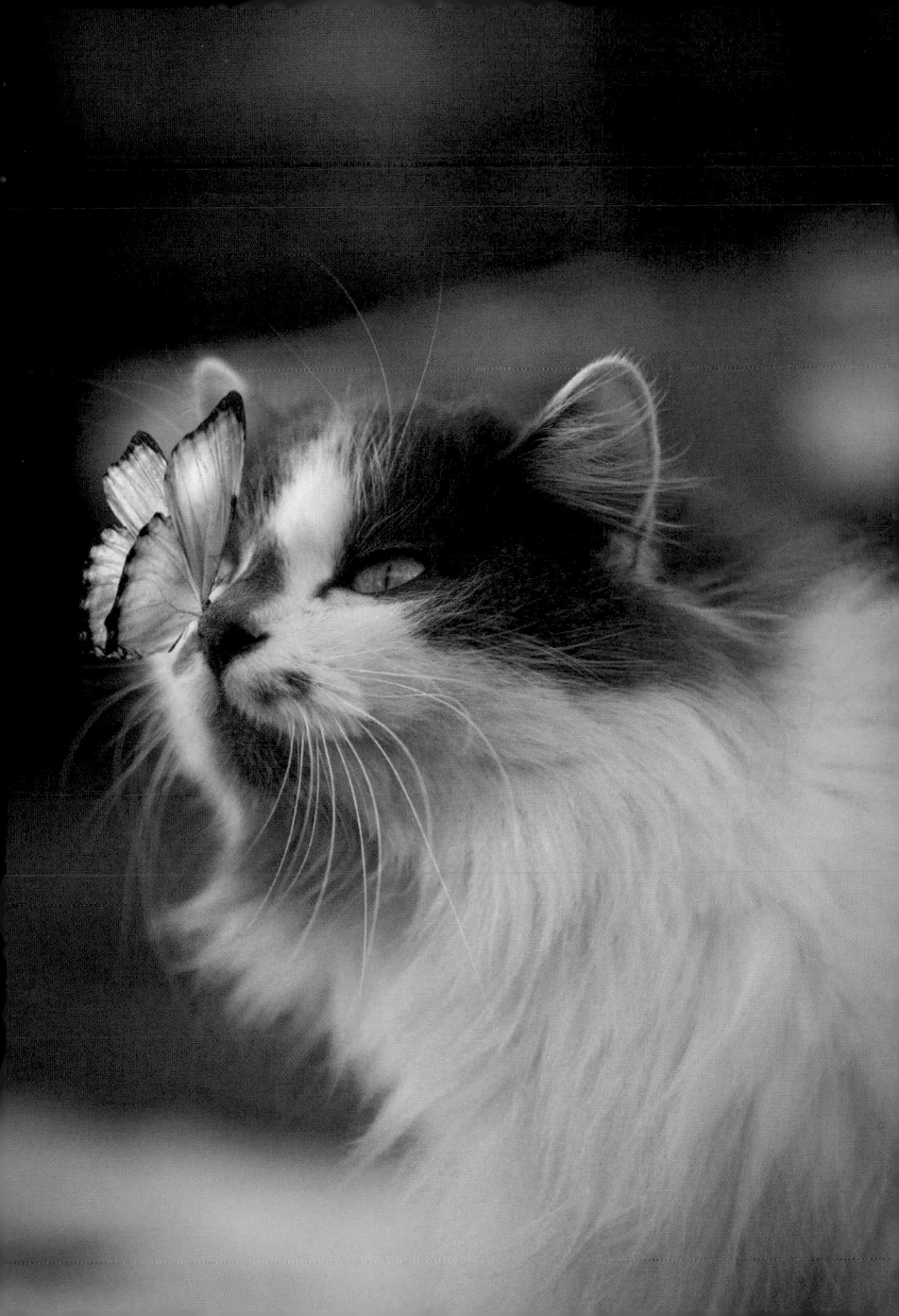

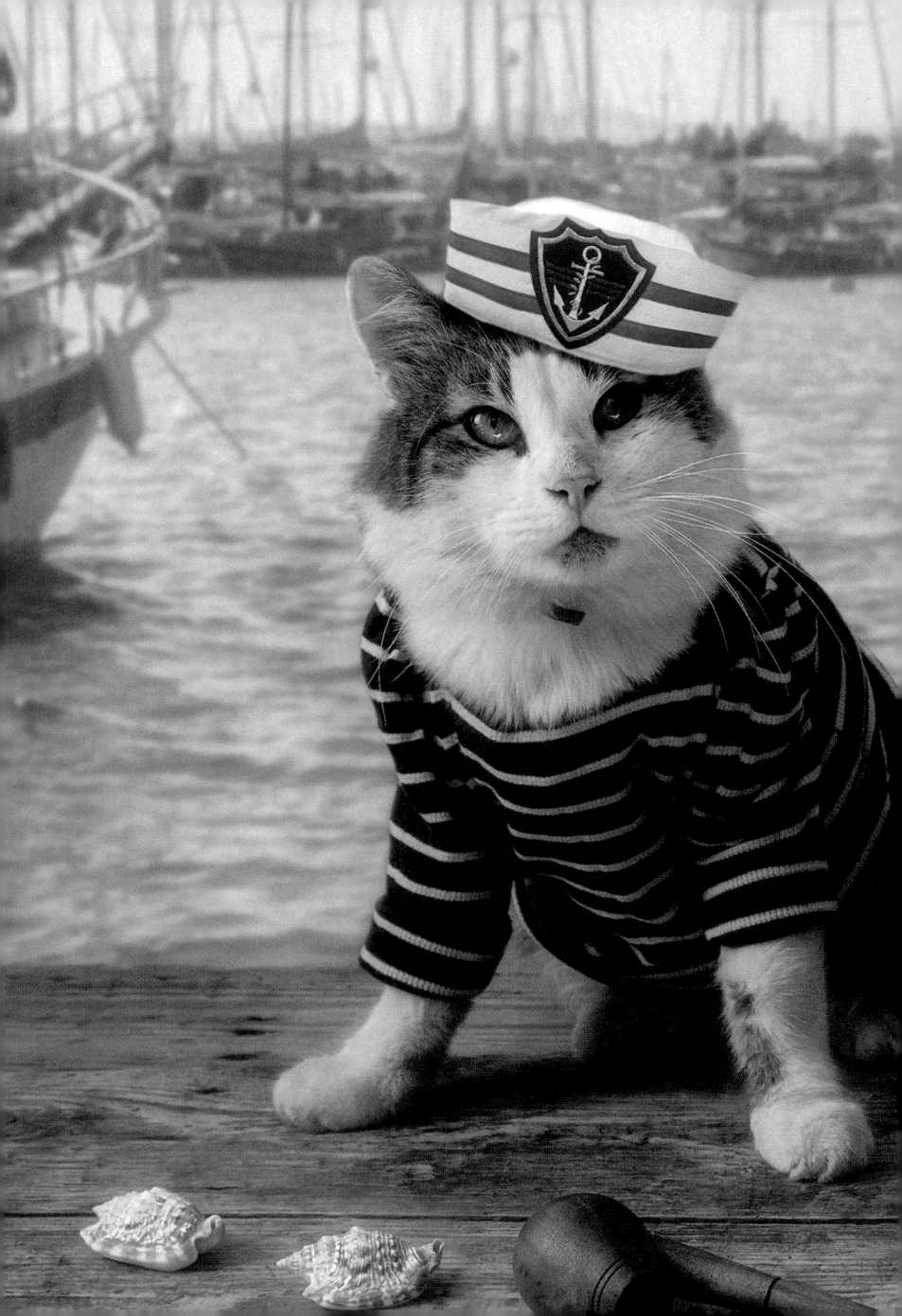

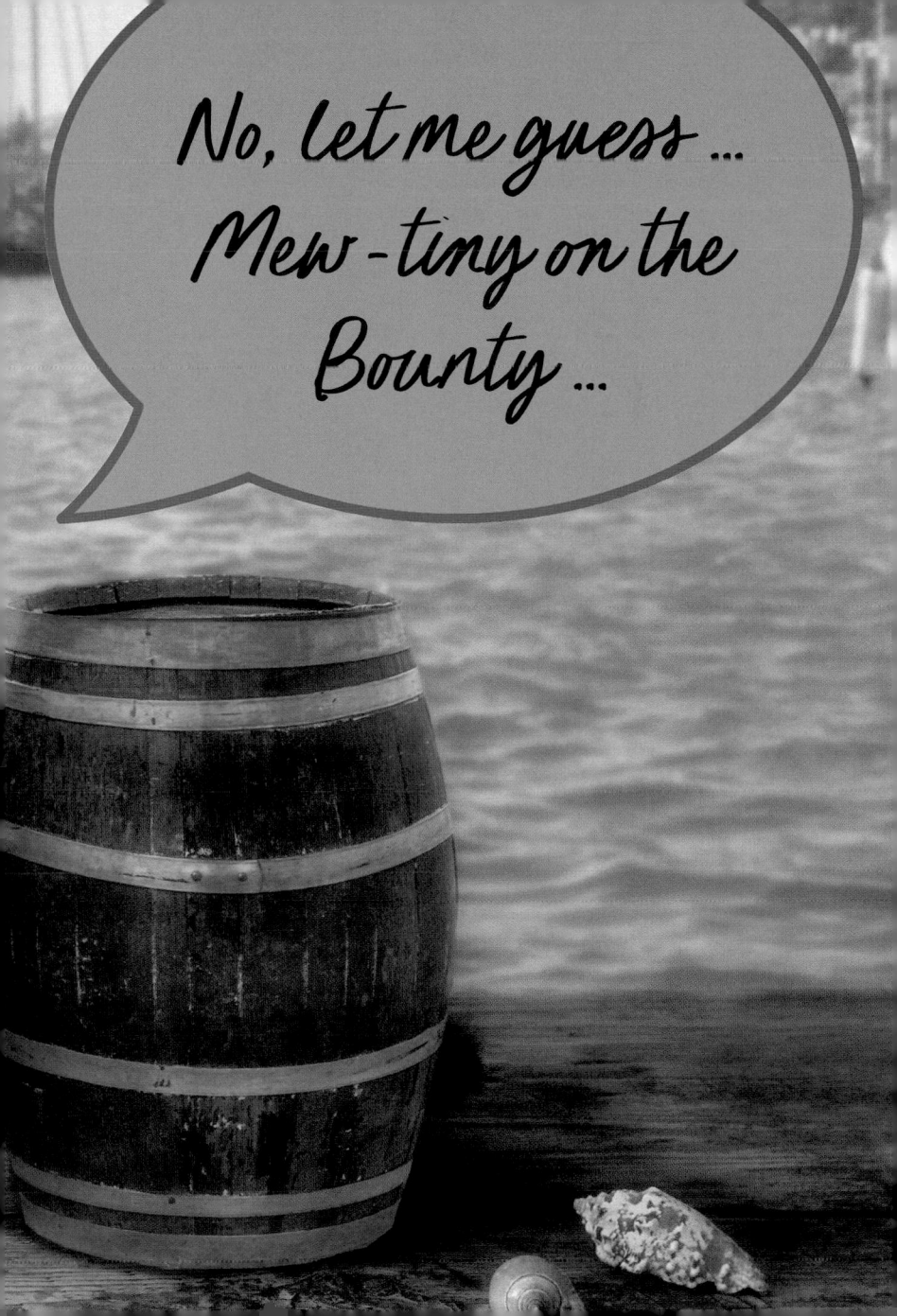
No, let me guess...
Mew-tiny on the
Bounty...

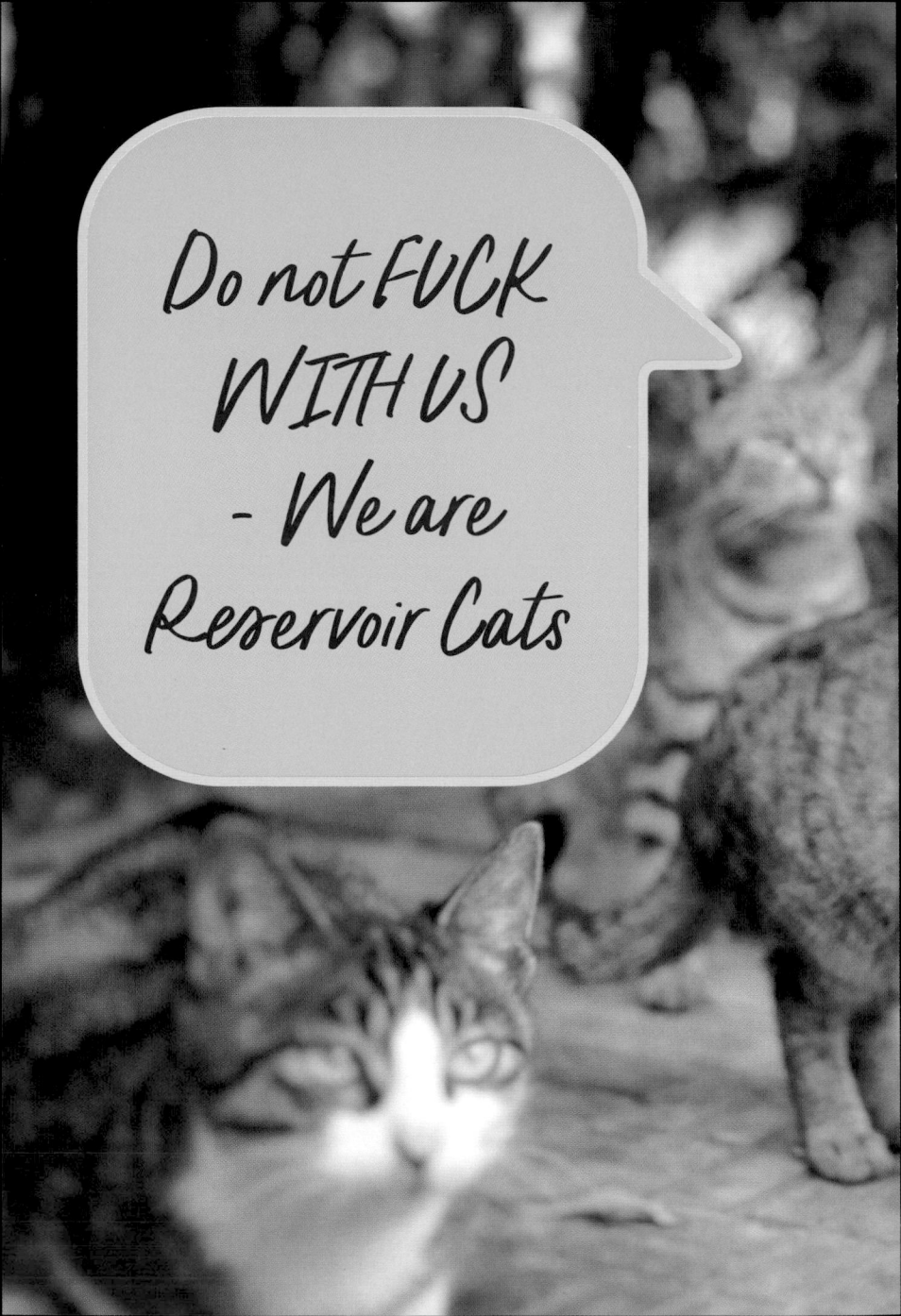
Do not FUCK
WITH US
- We are
Reservoir Cats

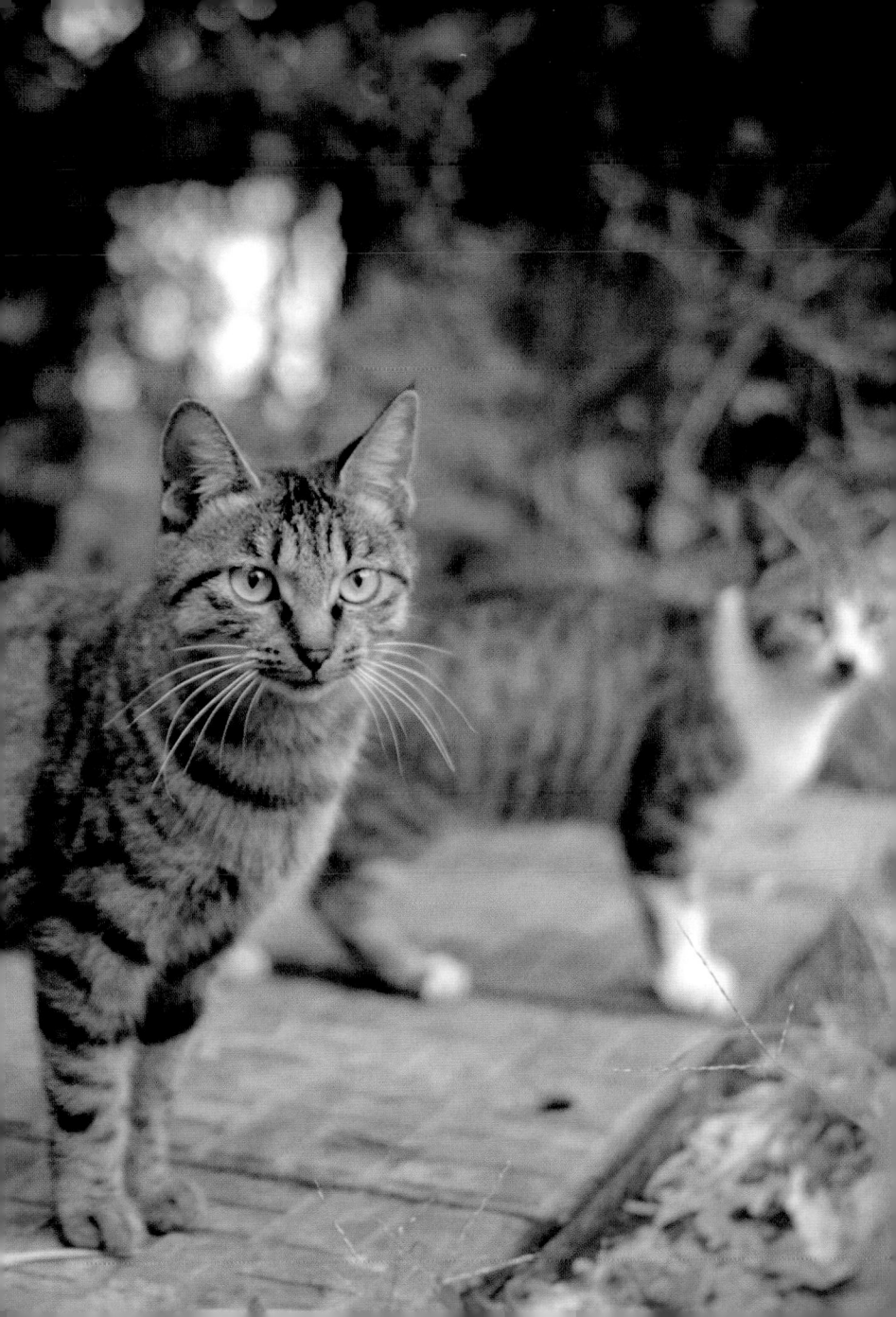

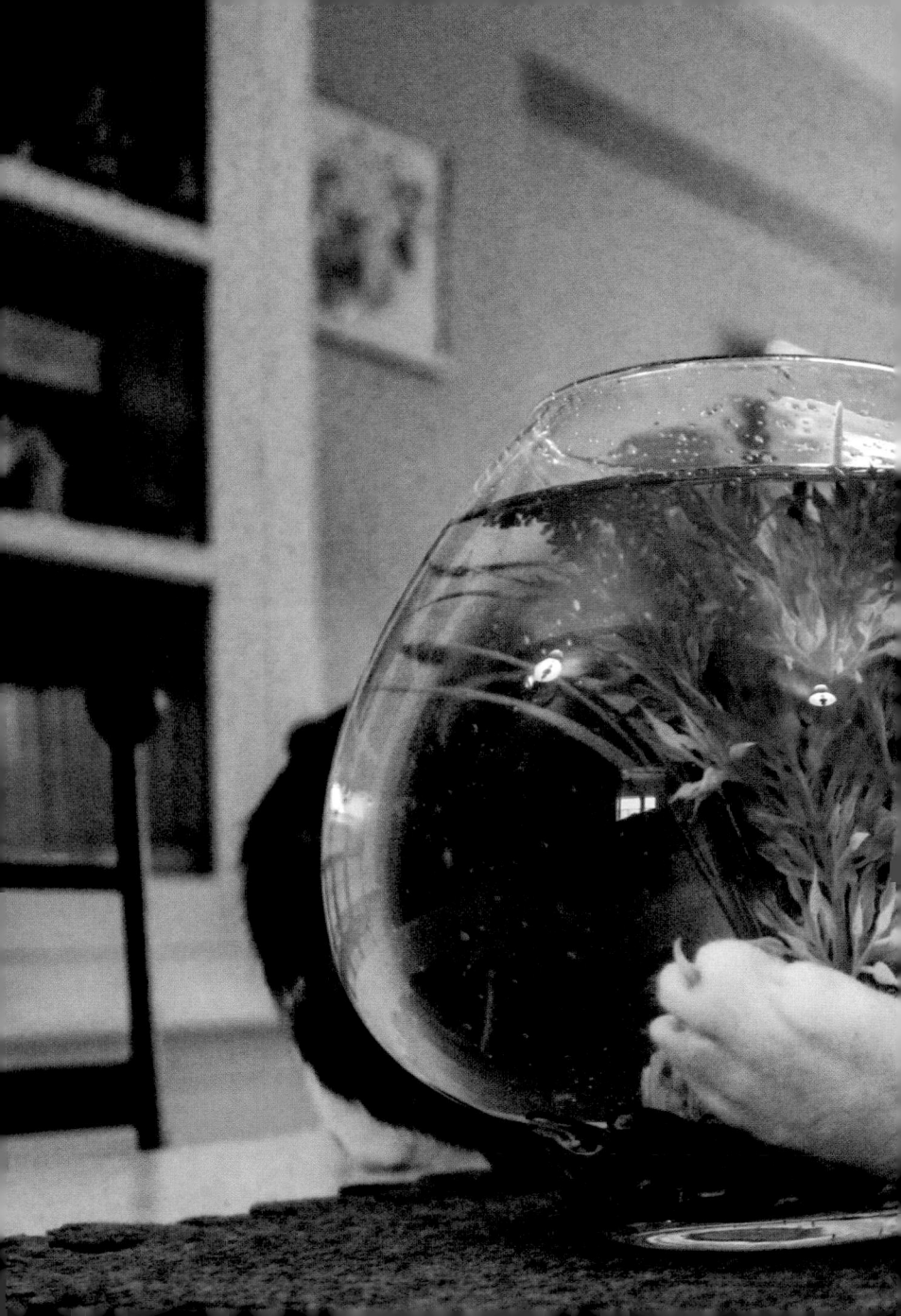

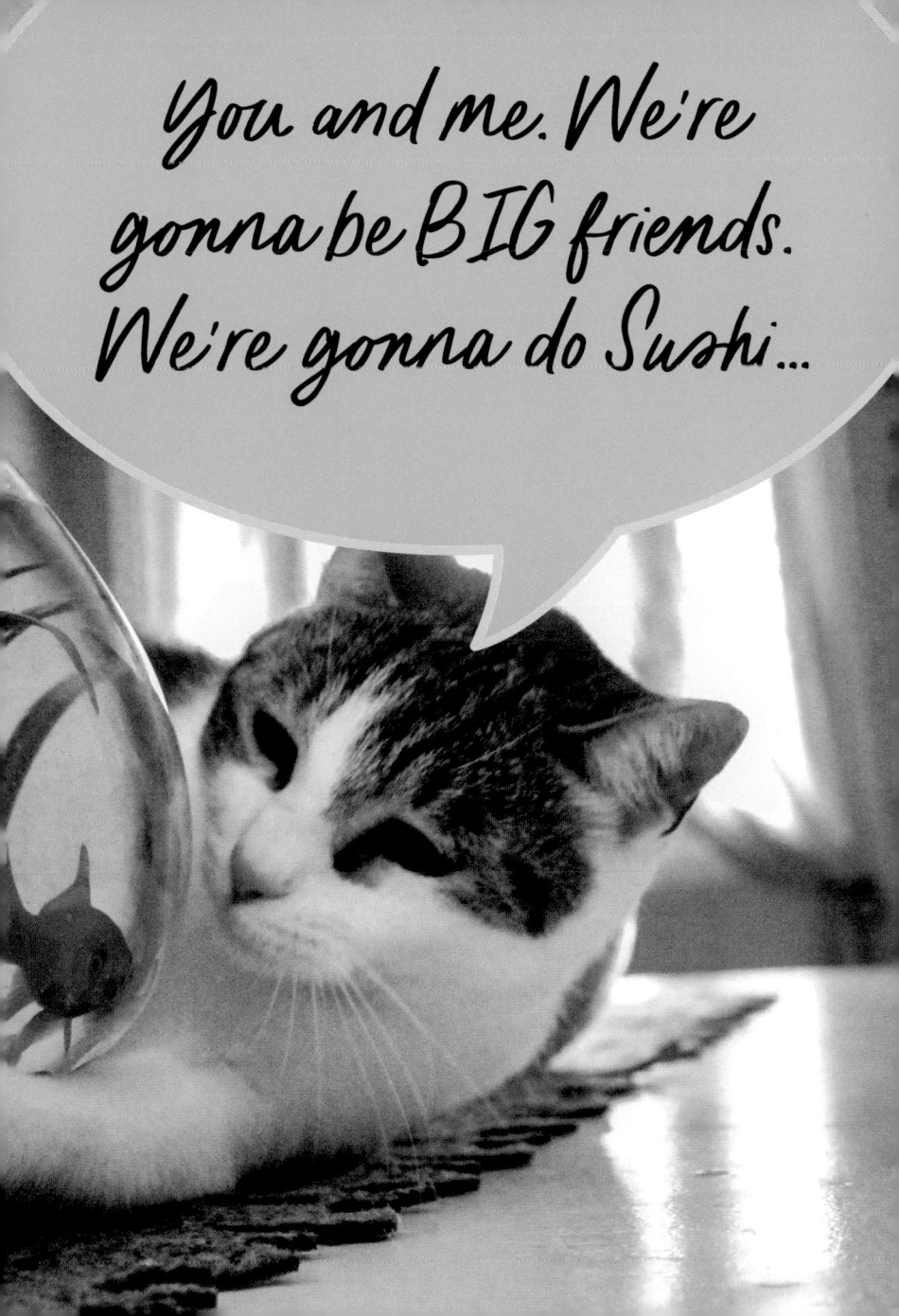
You and me. We're gonna be BIG friends. We're gonna do Sushi...

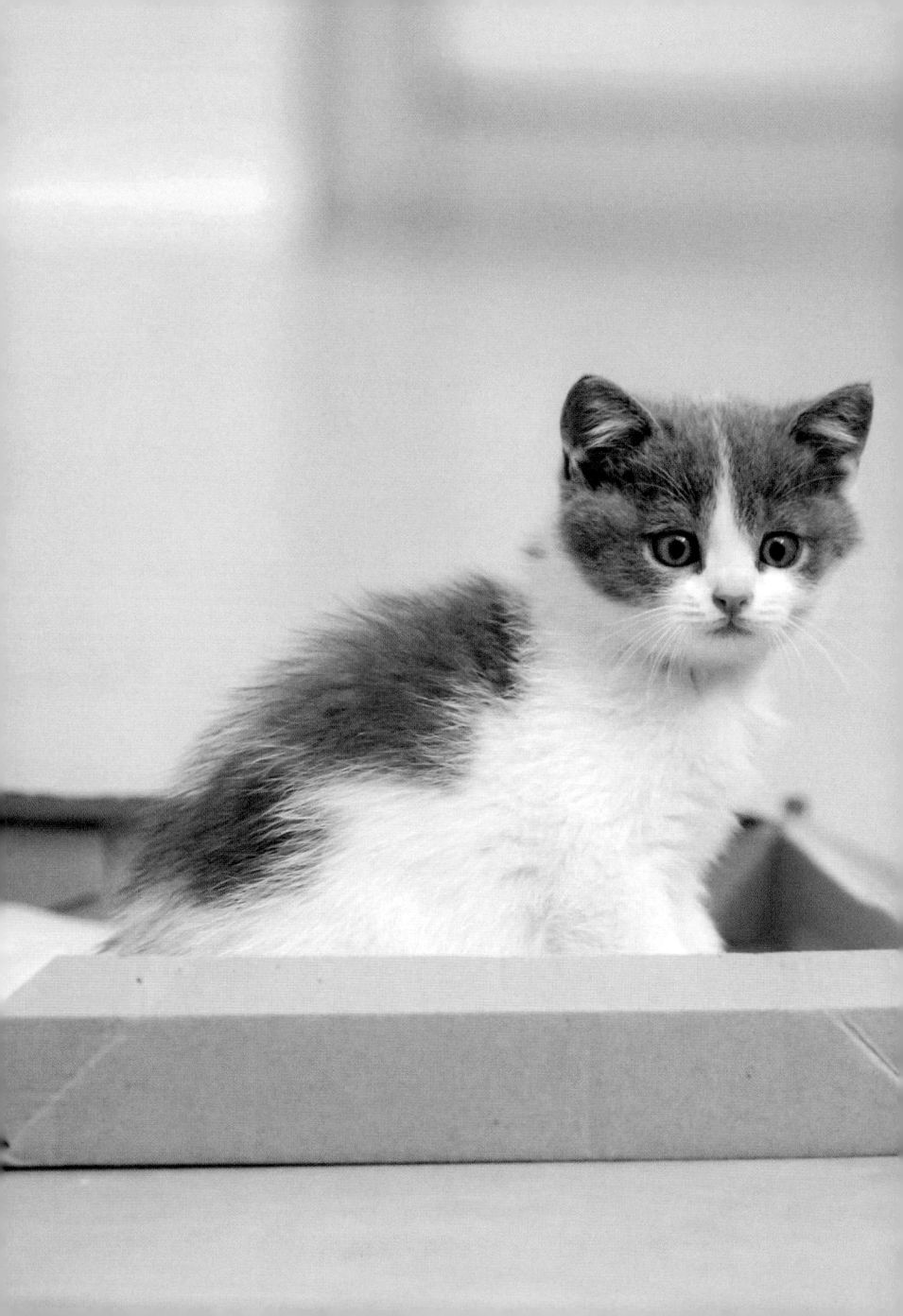

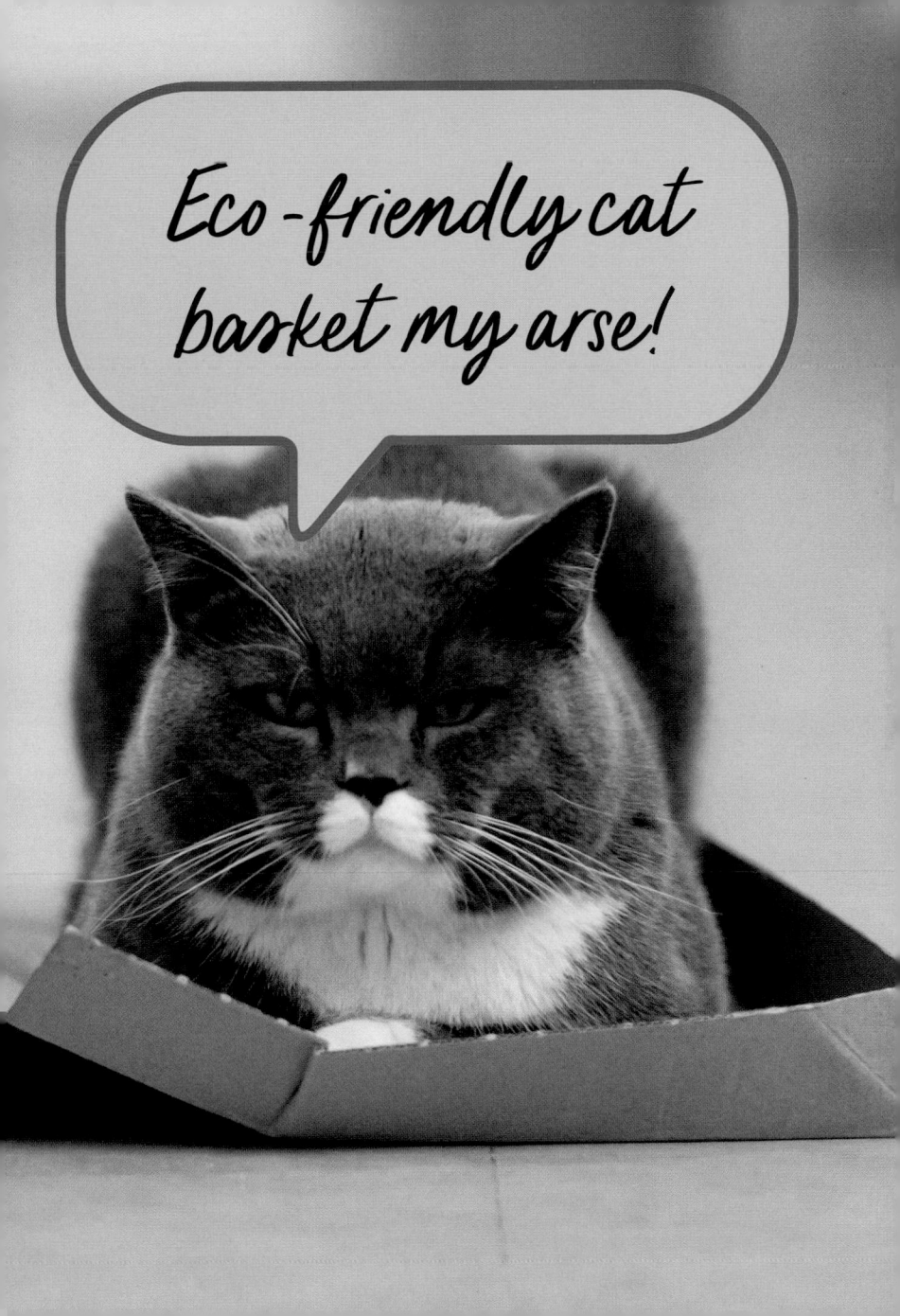
Eco-friendly cat
basket my arse!

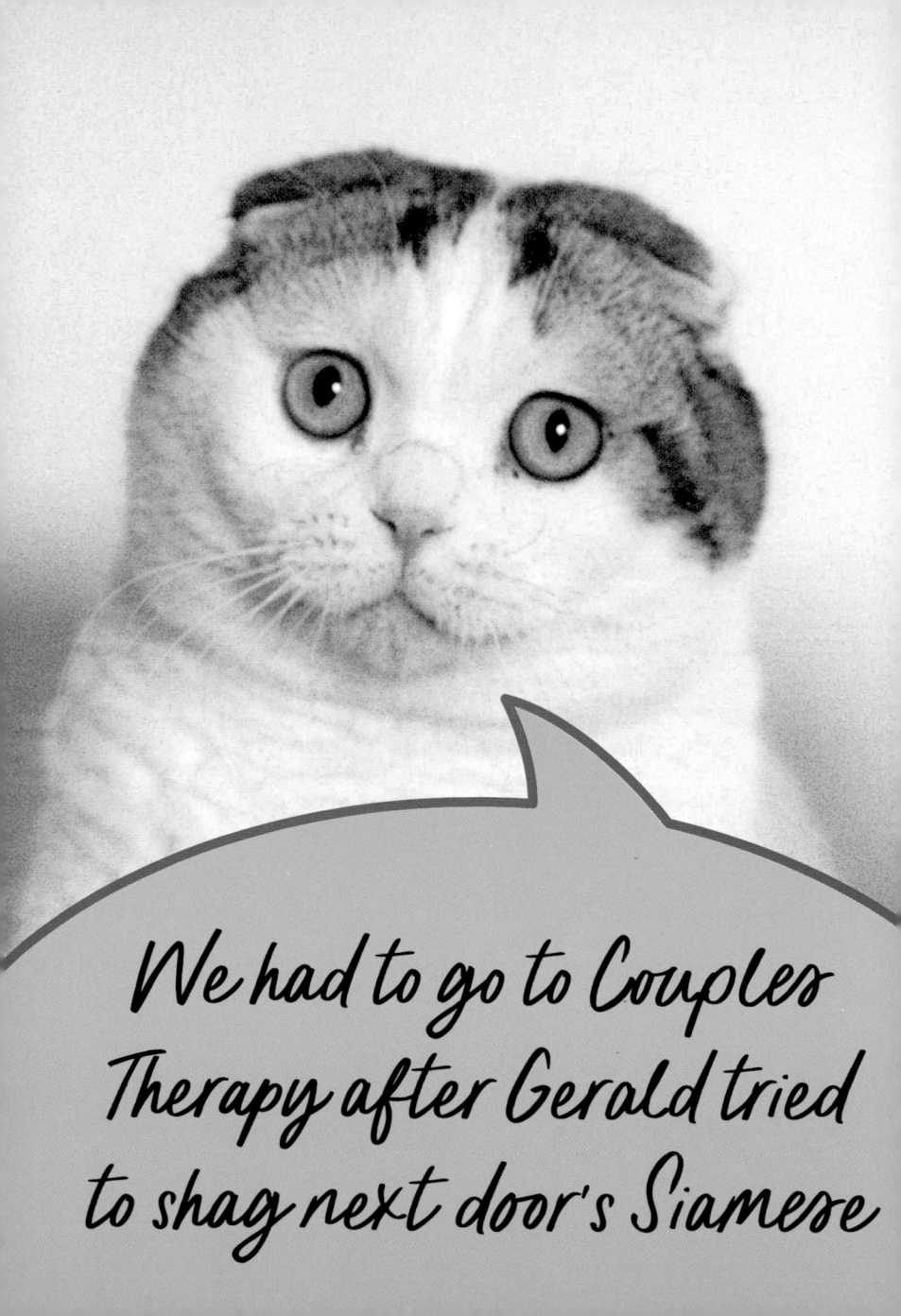
We had to go to Couples Therapy after Gerald tried to shag next door's Siamese

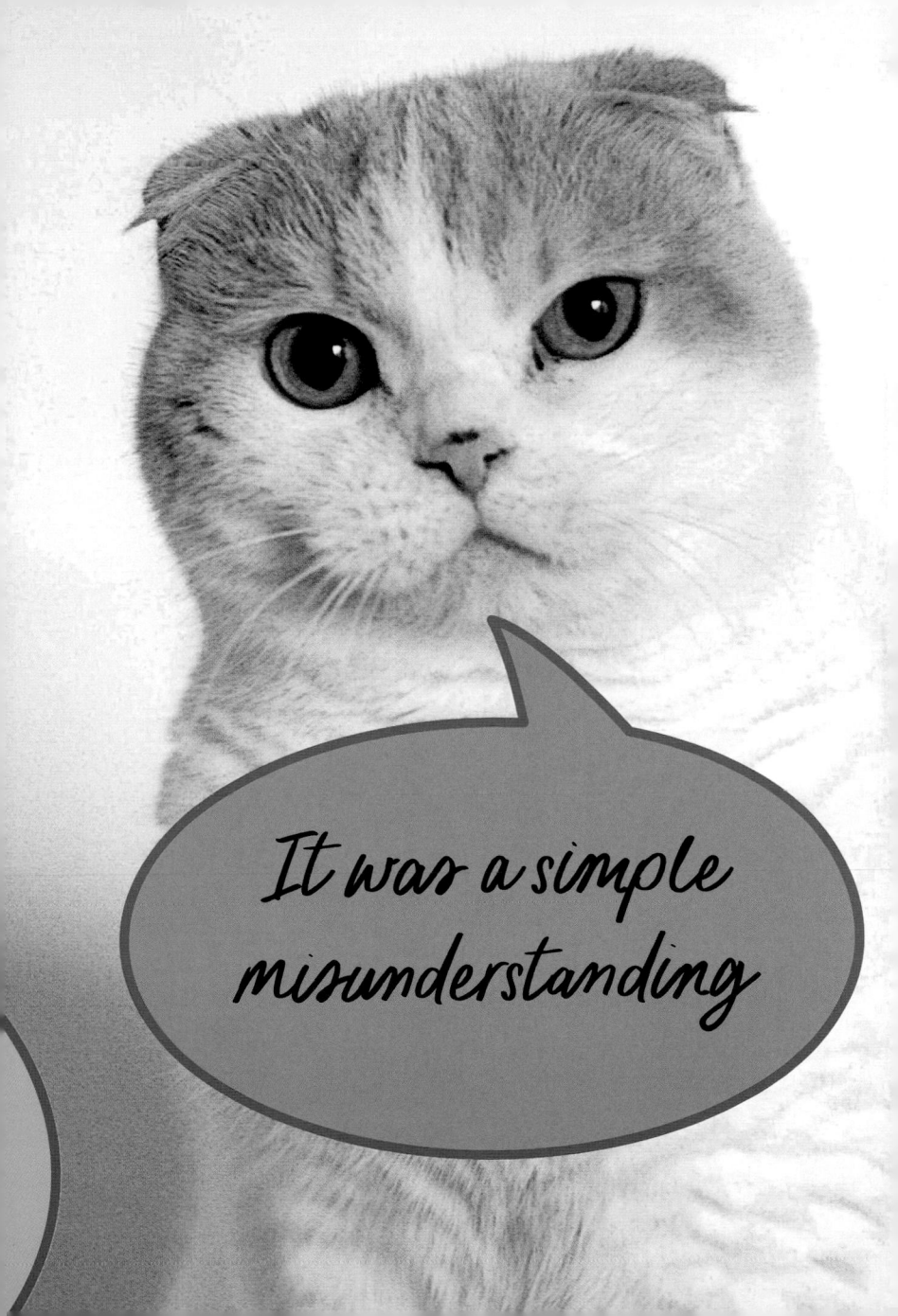
It was a simple misunderstanding

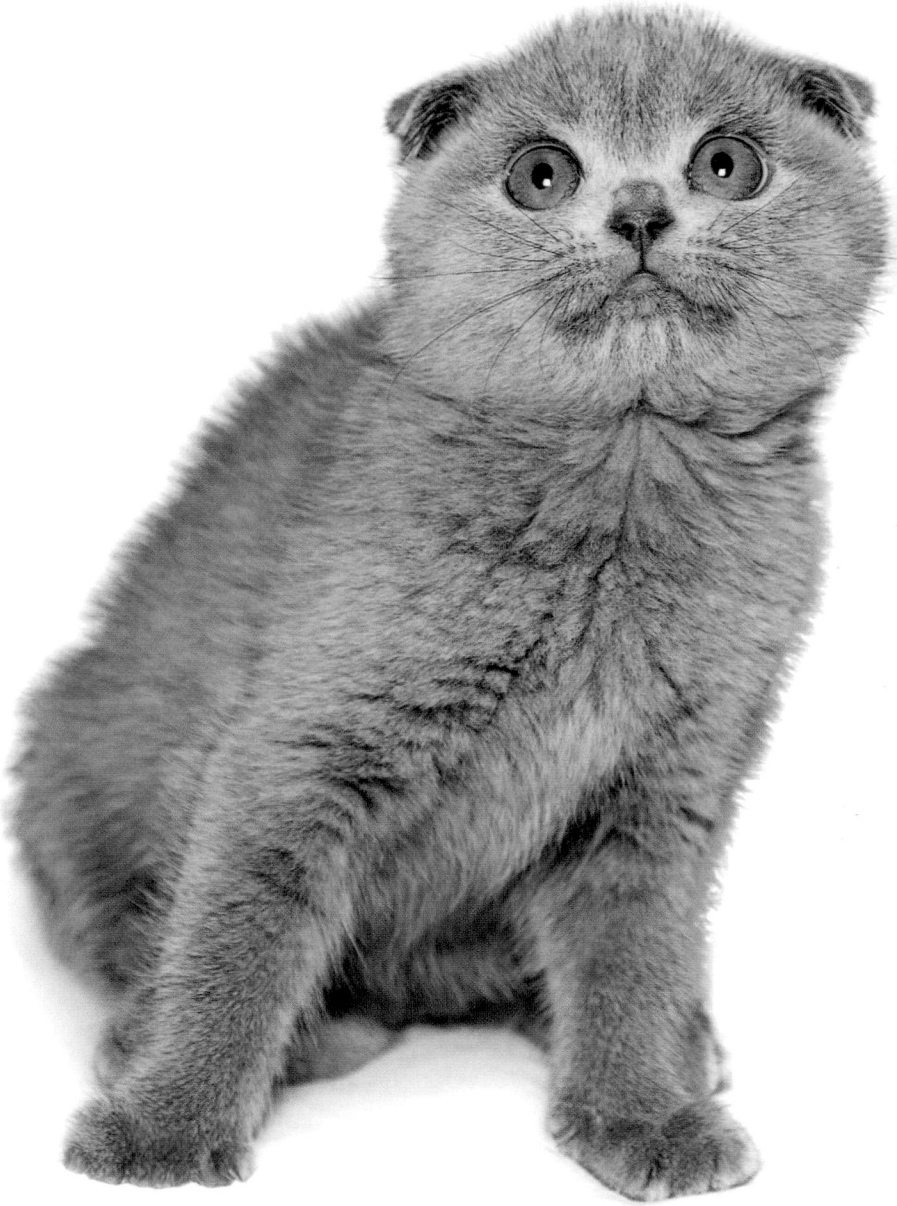

Wooaah! What's she doing with that wax strip...?

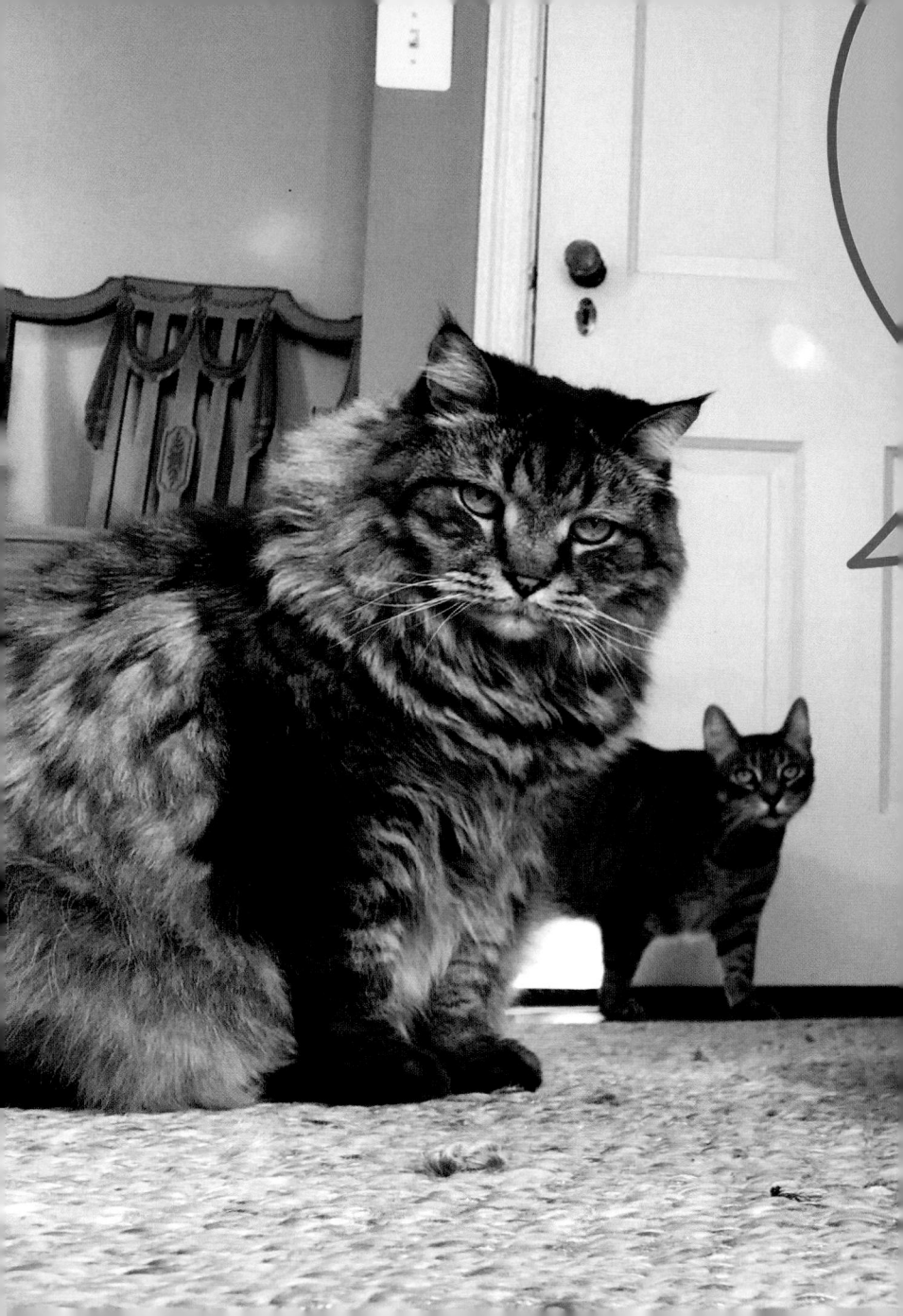

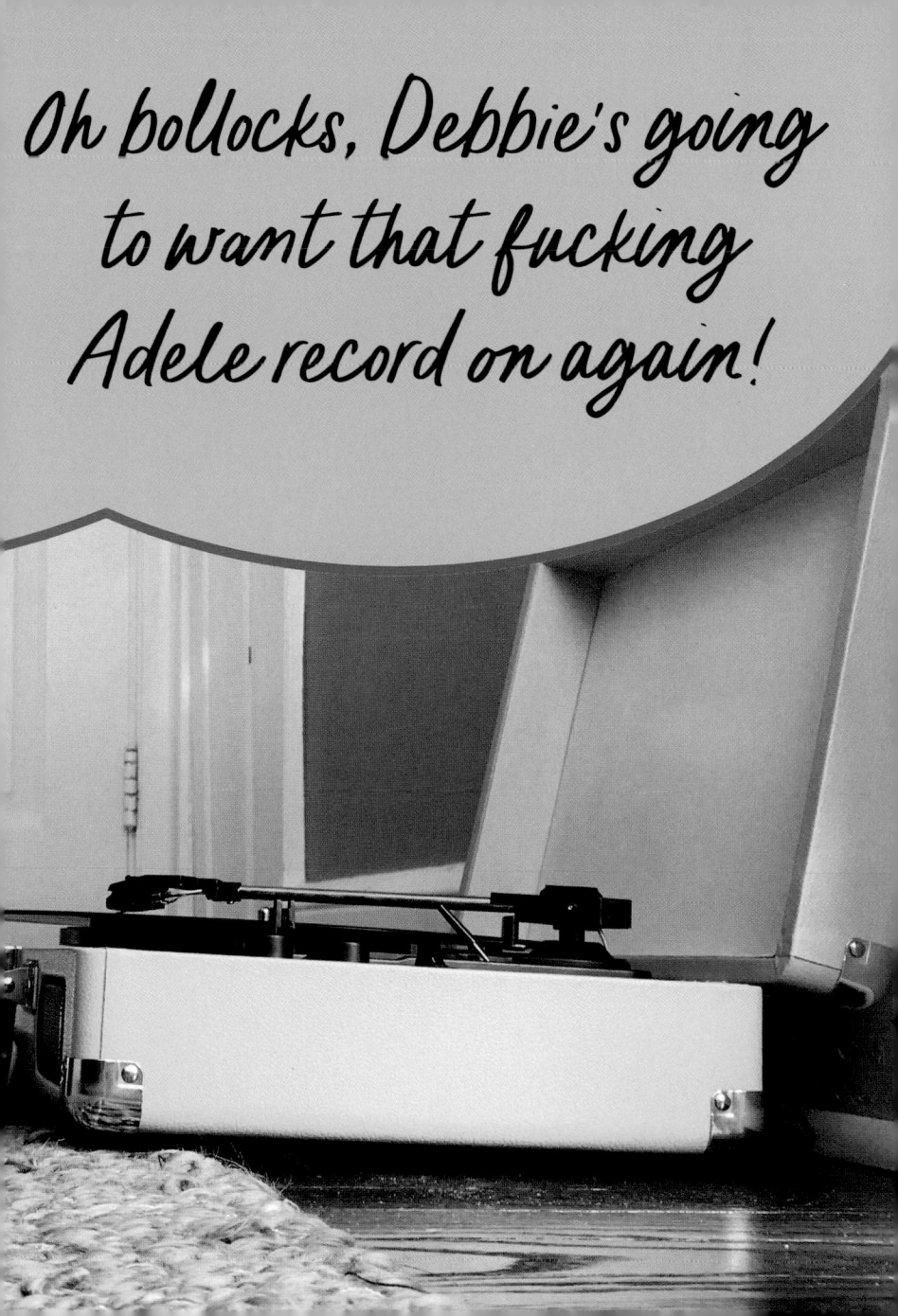
Oh bollocks, Debbie's going to want that fucking Adele record on again!

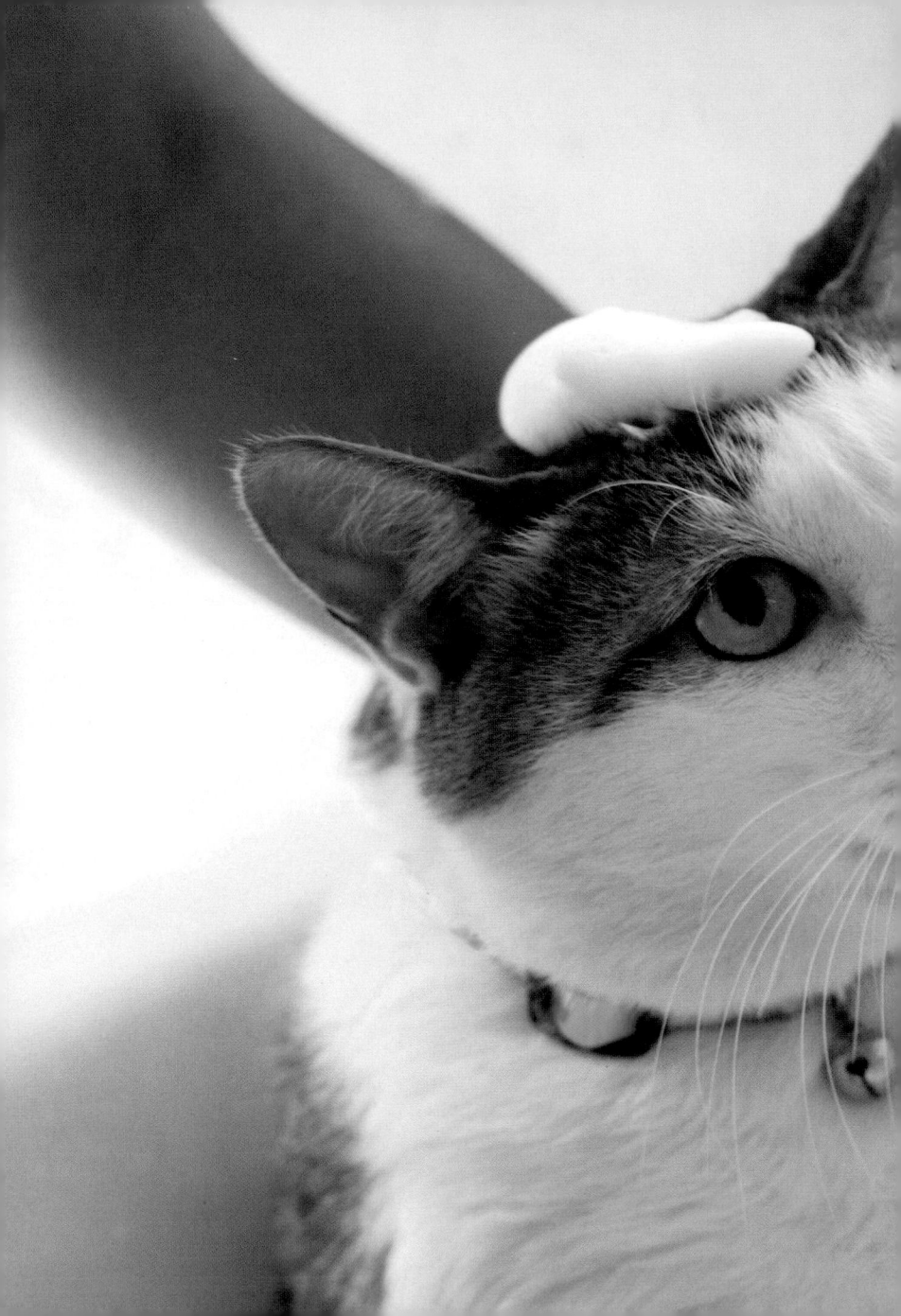

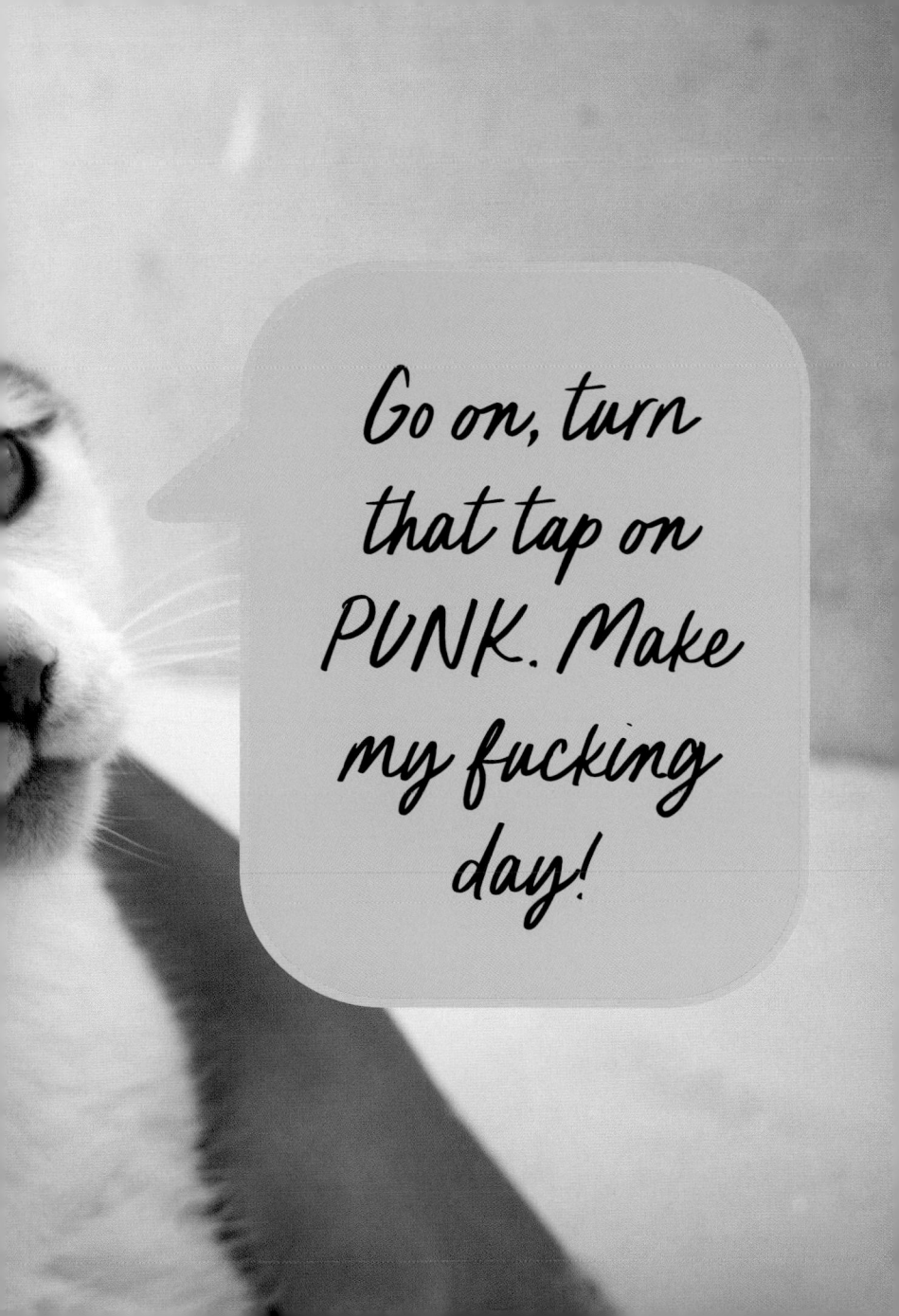
Go on, turn that tap on PUNK. Make my fucking day!

This one's for my
OnlyFans site

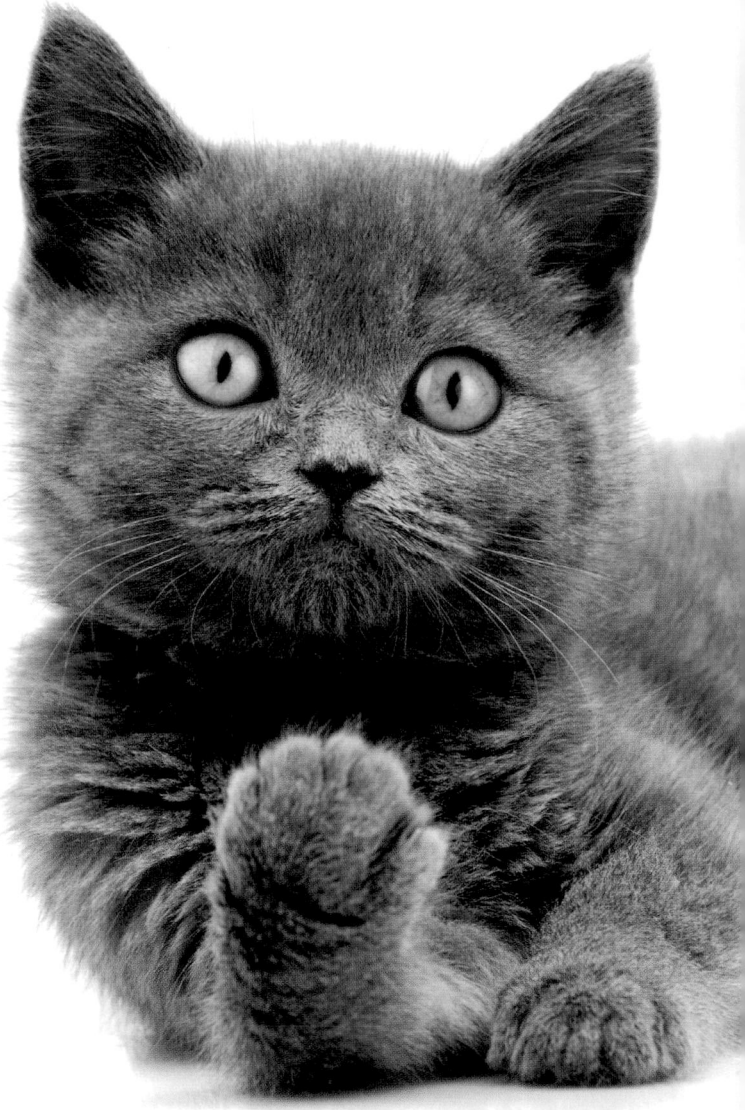

Did you just say "TIDY UP YOUR BEDROOM...?"

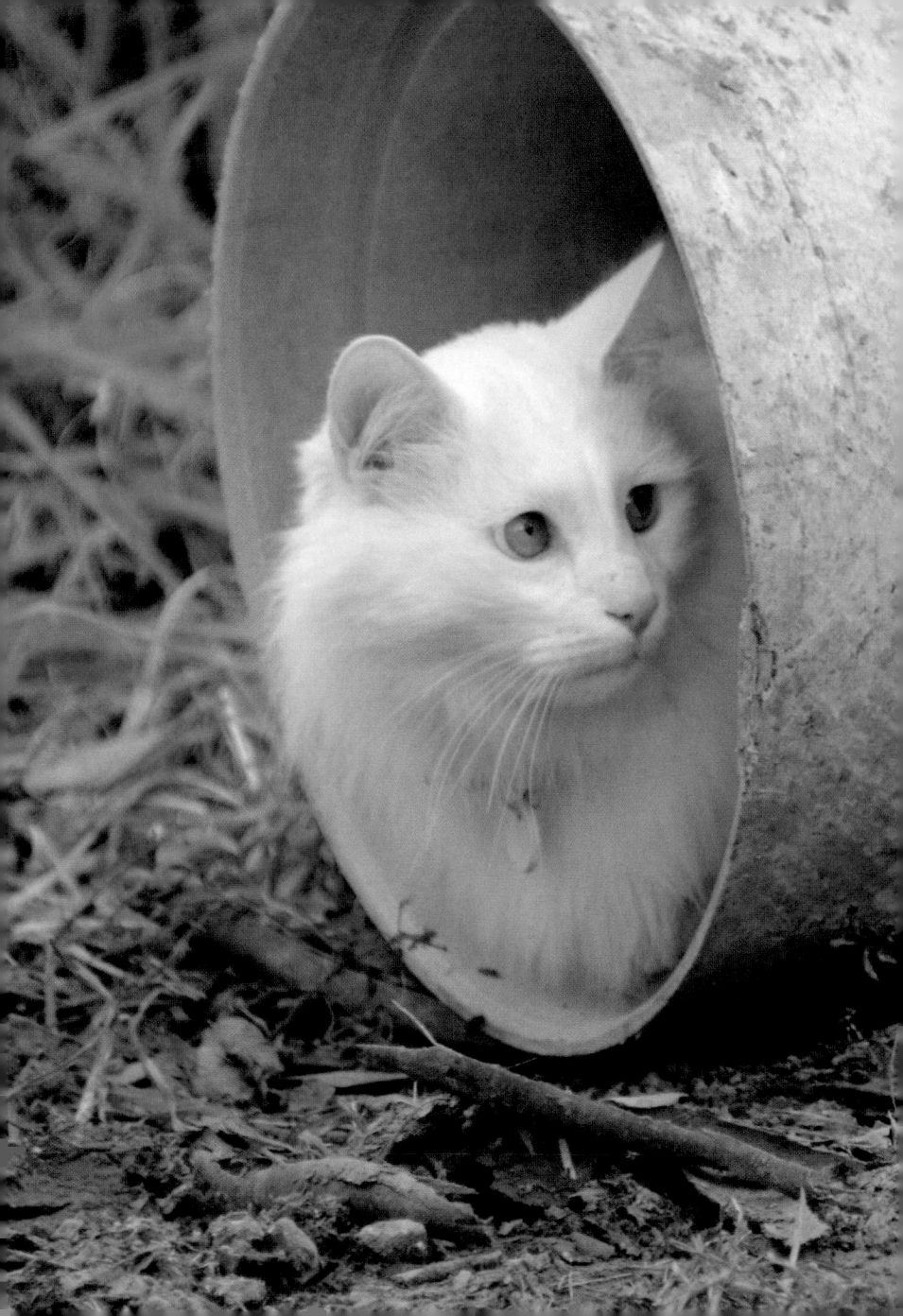

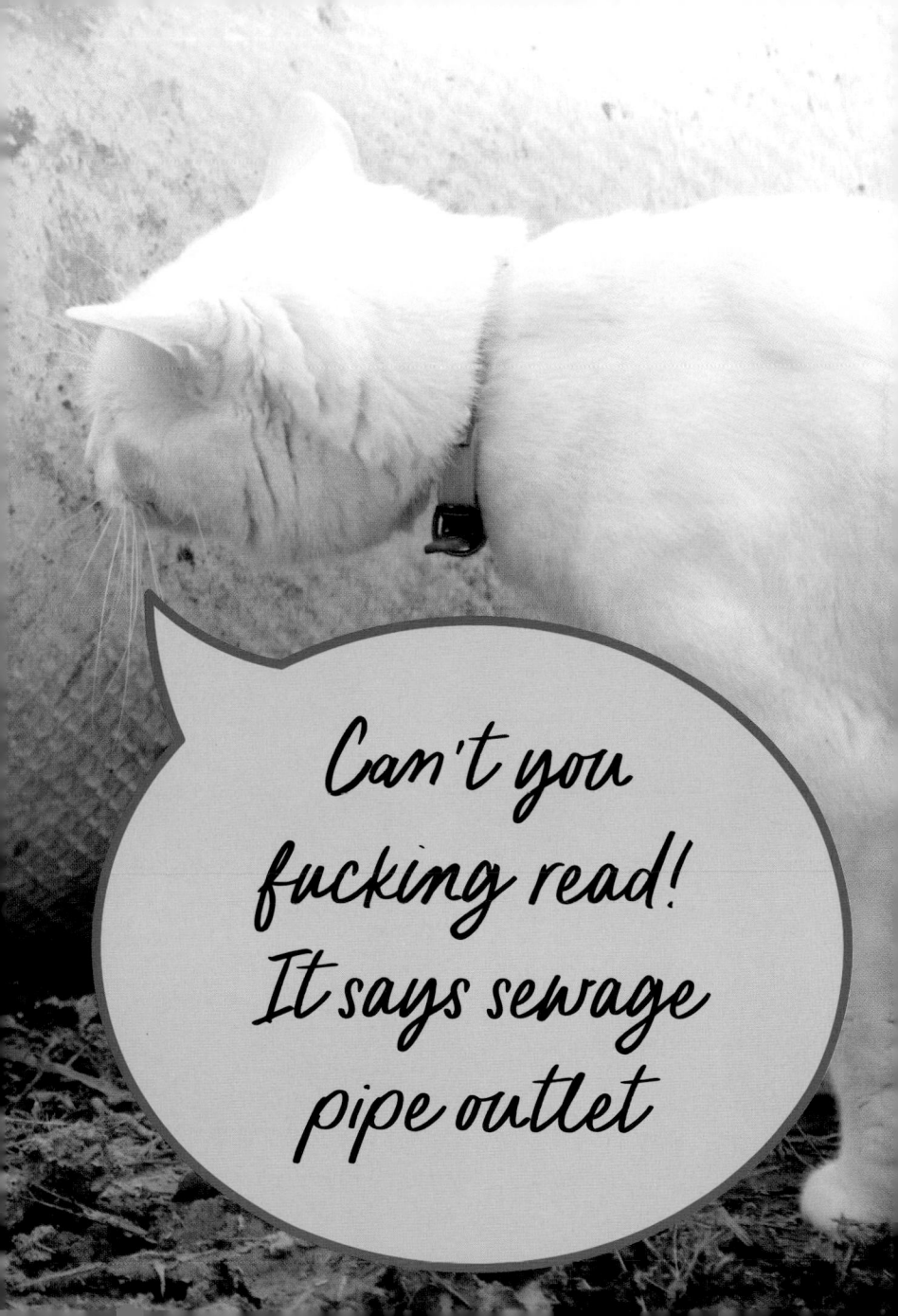
Can't you fucking read! It says sewage pipe outlet

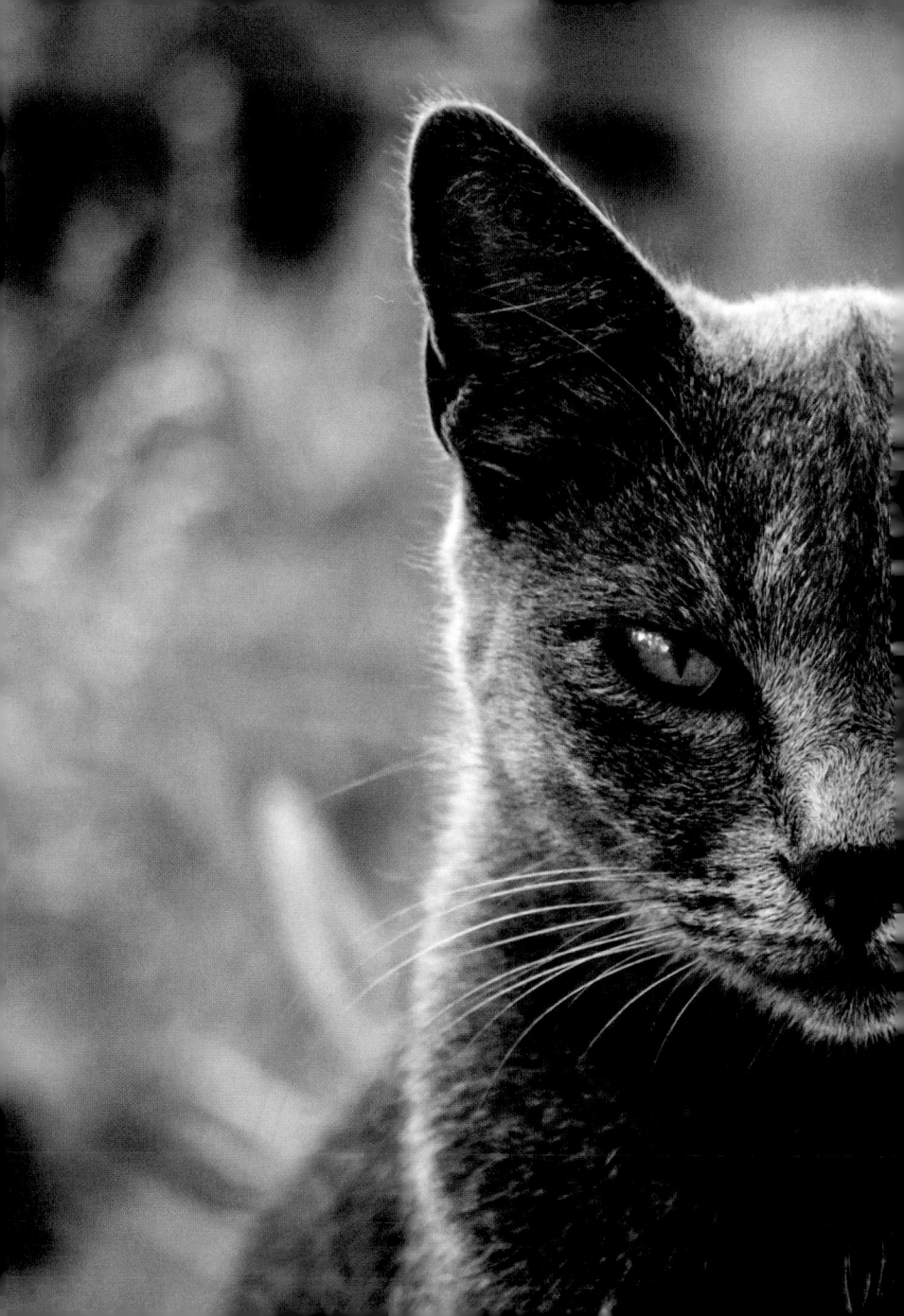

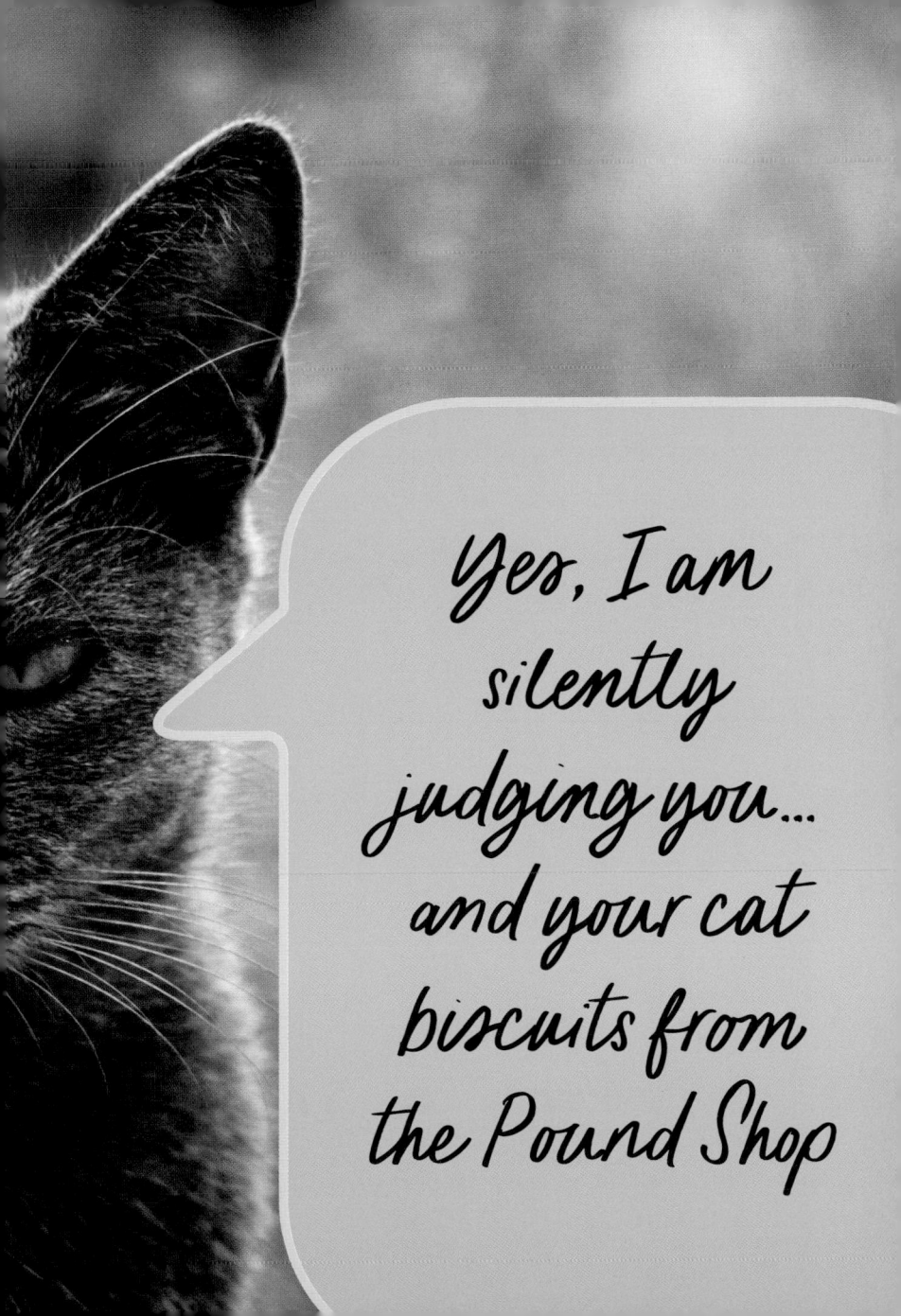
Yes, I am silently judging you... and your cat biscuits from the Pound Shop

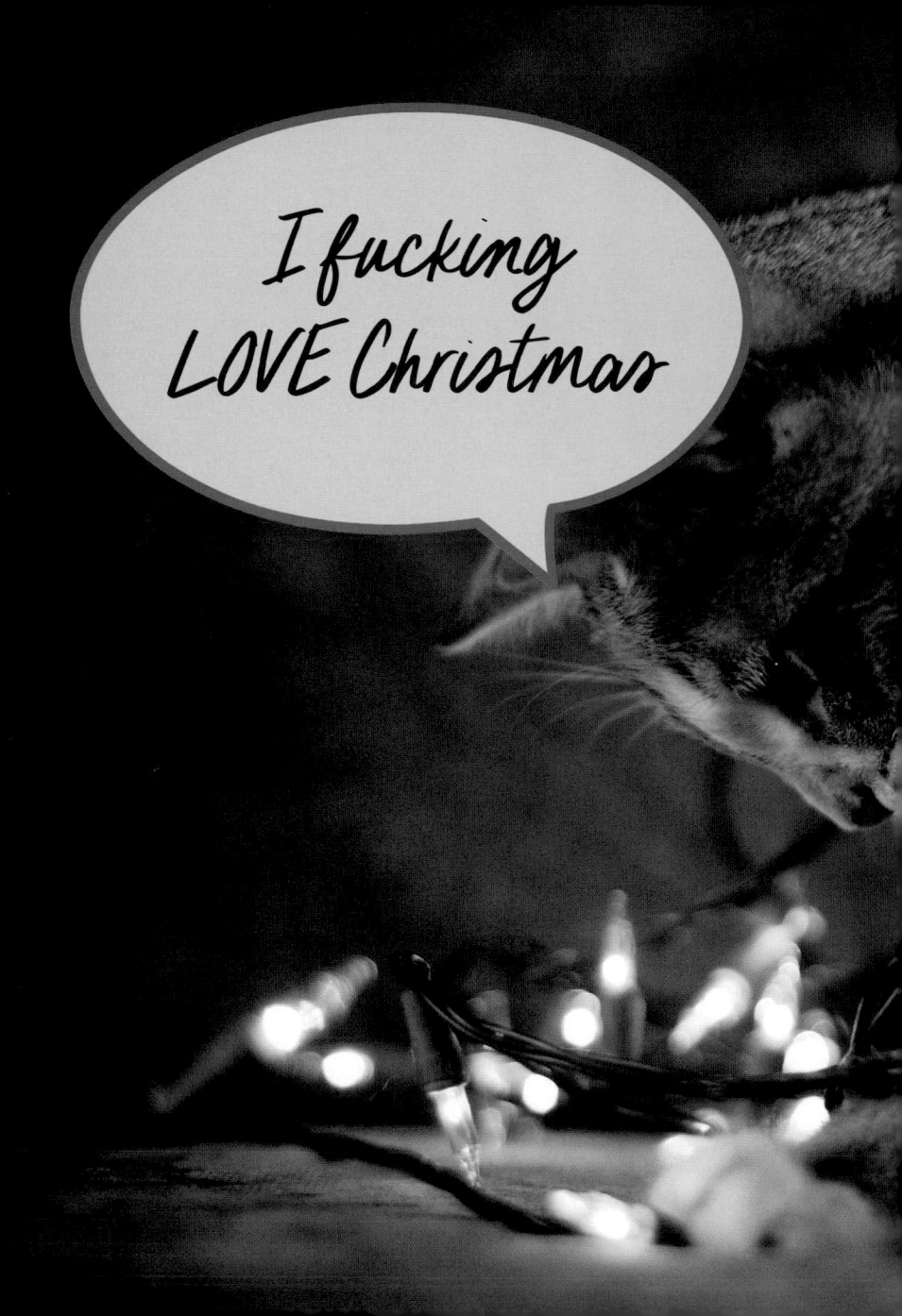
I fucking
LOVE Christmas

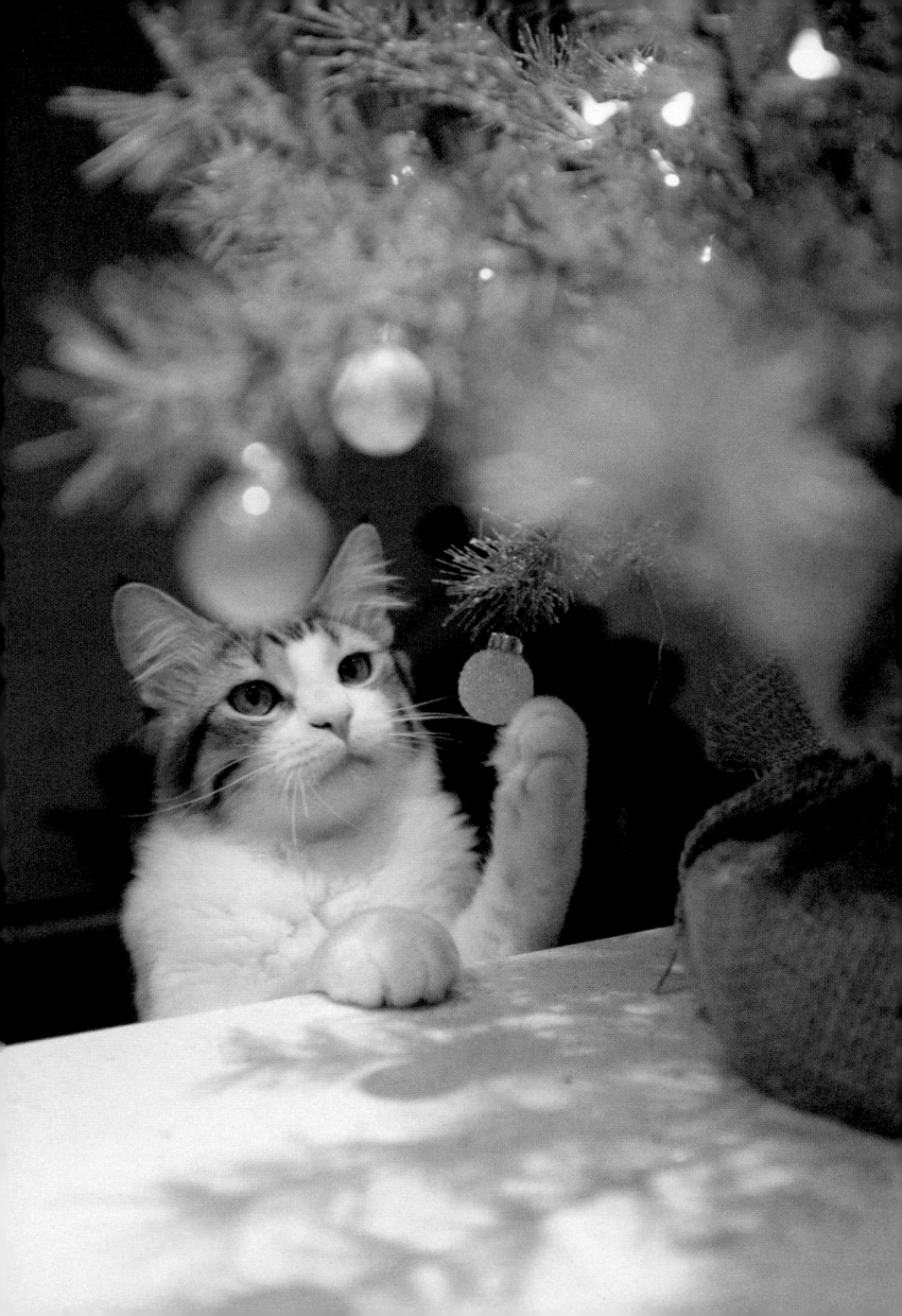

Aaaaw, 'Pussy's first Xmas' and the DIMSHITS have left all the baubles within reach...

Have you just put YOUR SKANKY PANTs on MY head...?

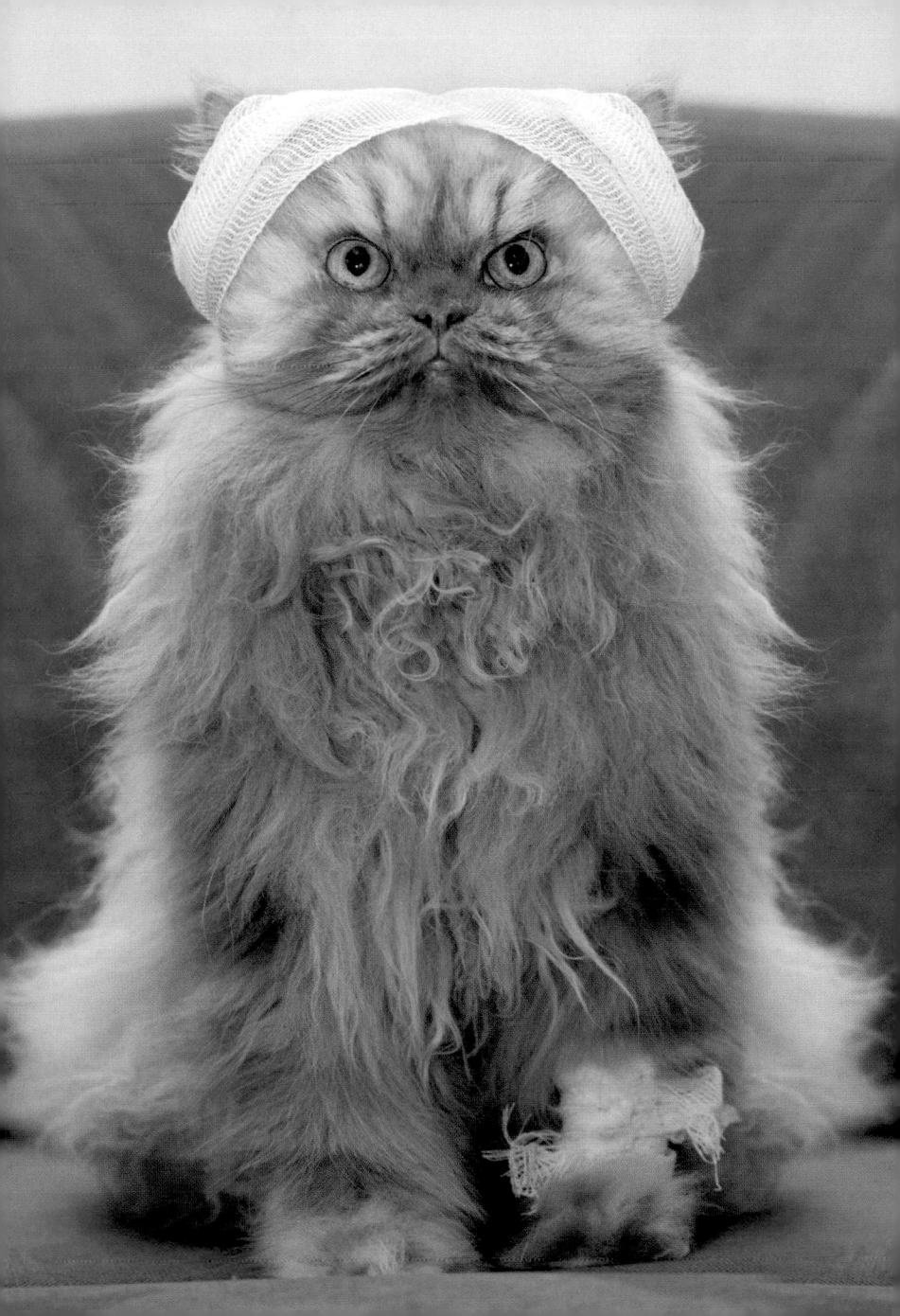

No, I'm not a big, grey, friendly rabbit. I'm a big nasty cat. And you are buggered

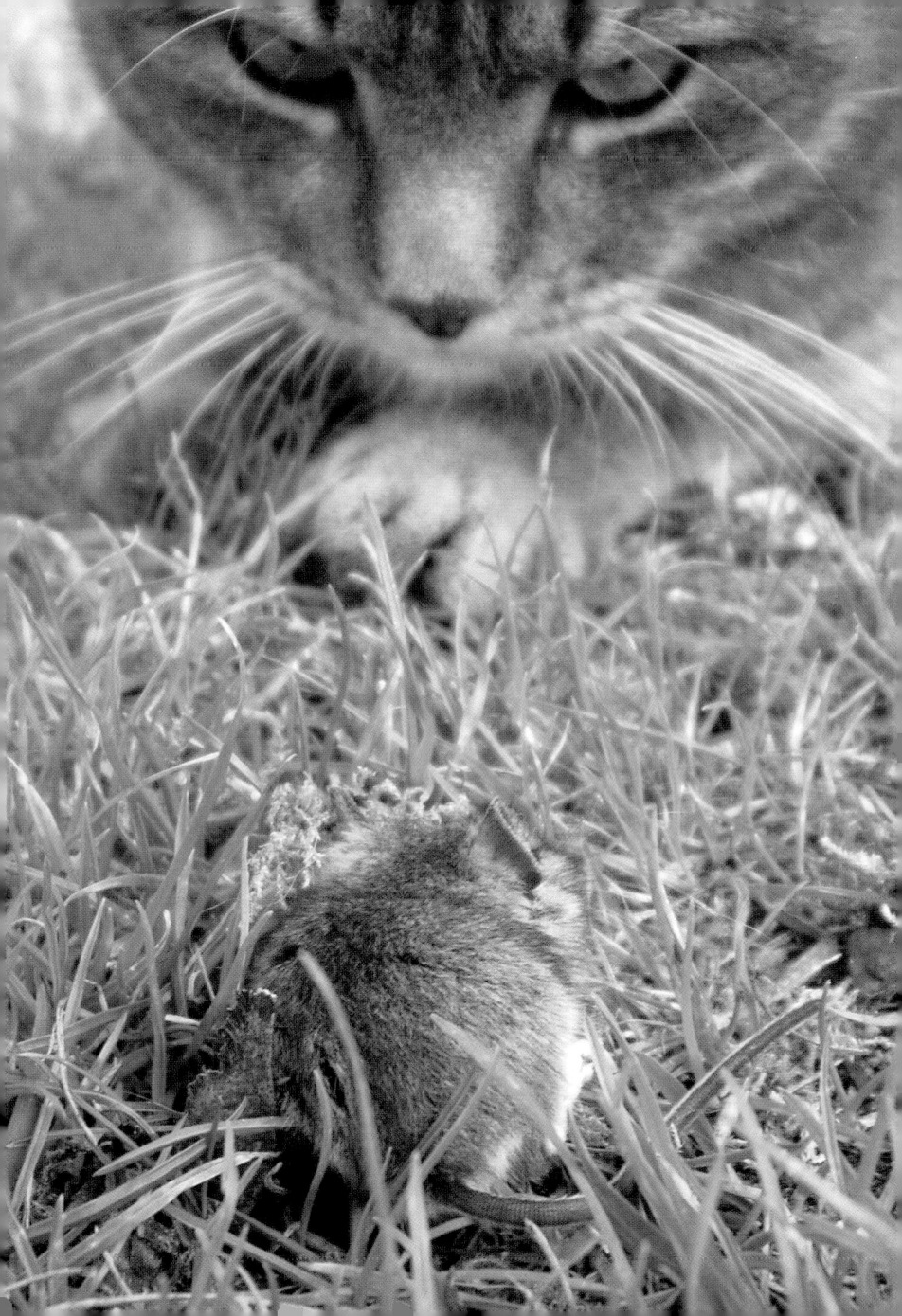

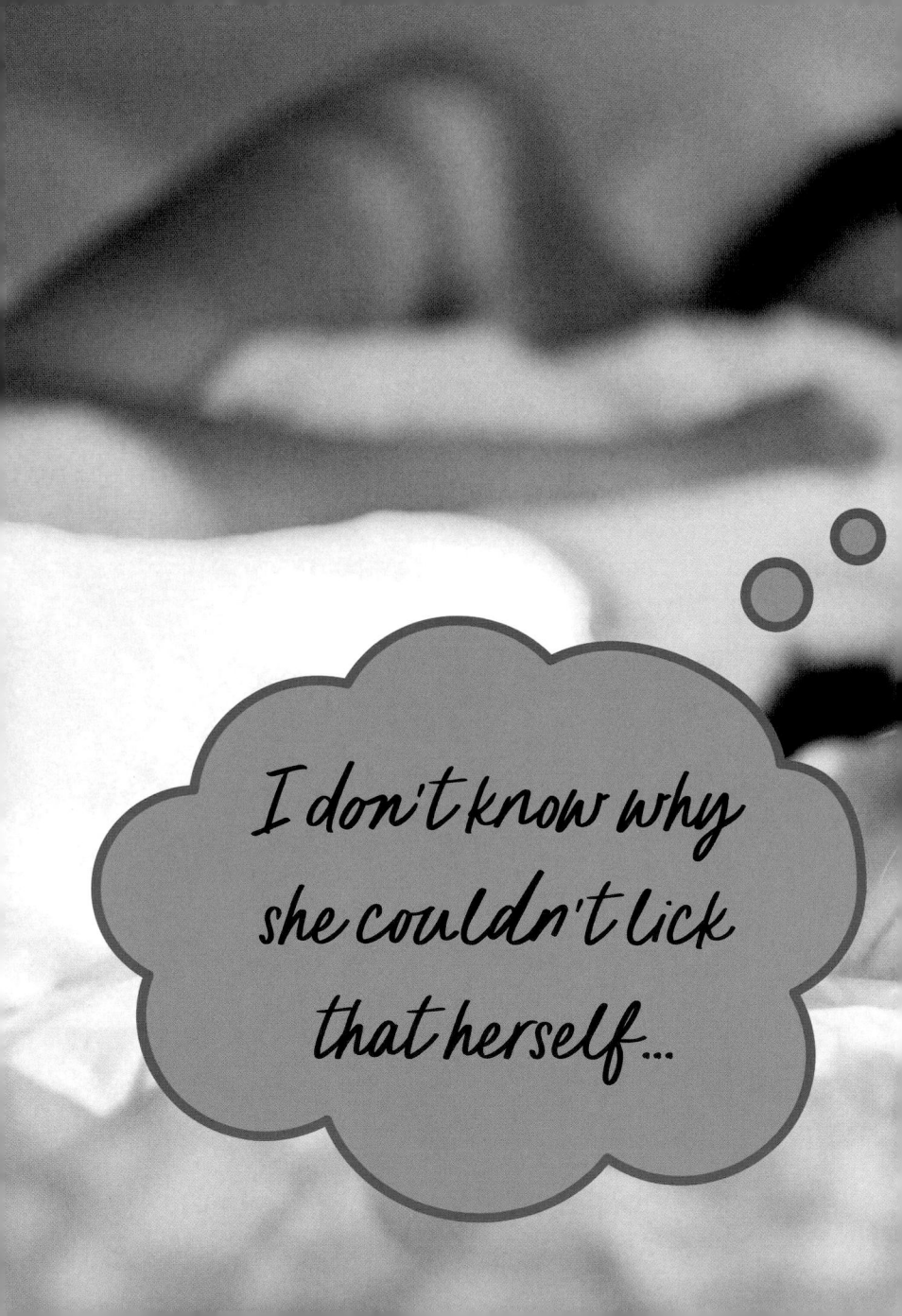
I don't know why
she couldn't lick
that herself...

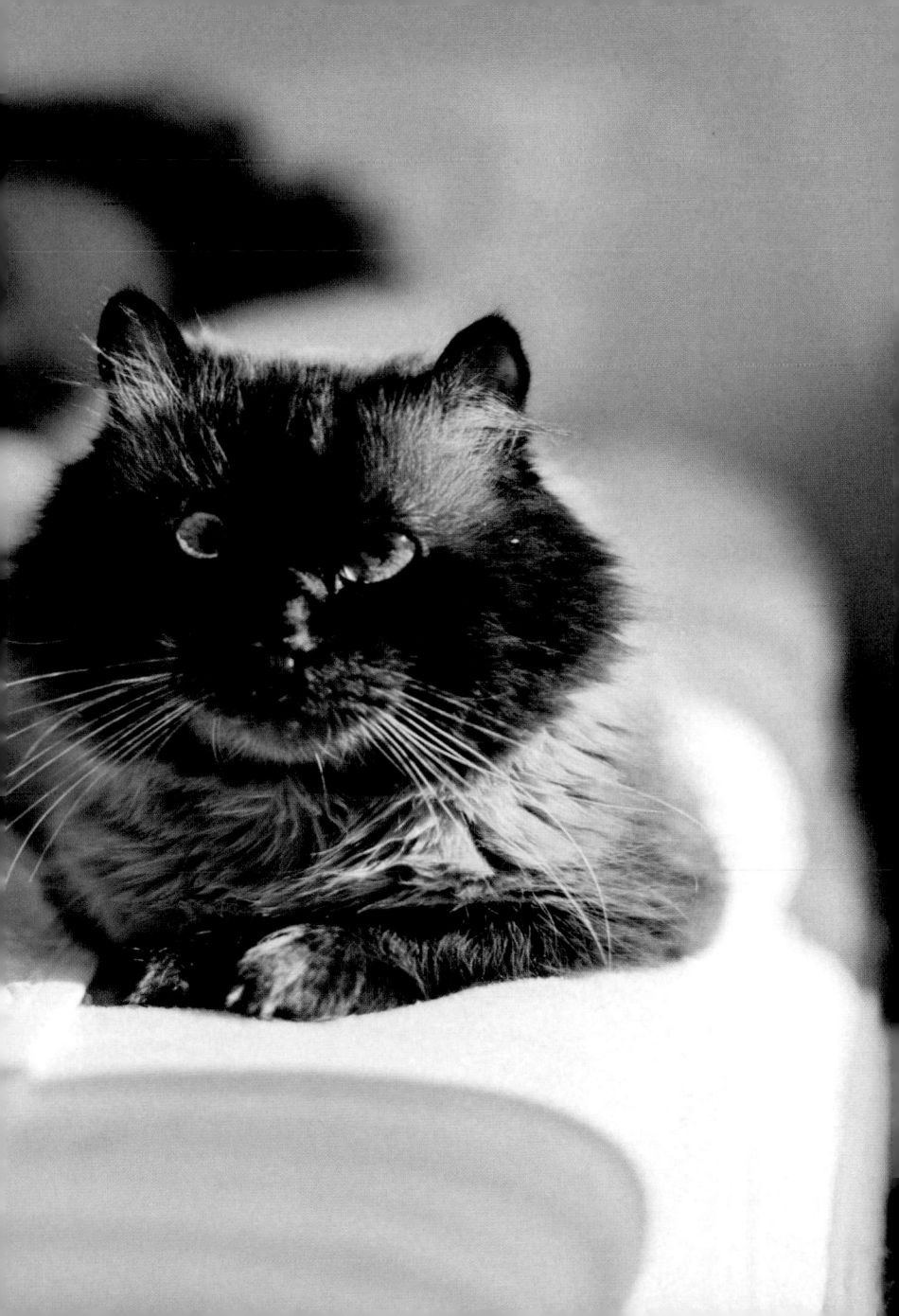

No George Clarke,
this isn't
AMAAAAAZING.
It's a shitbox

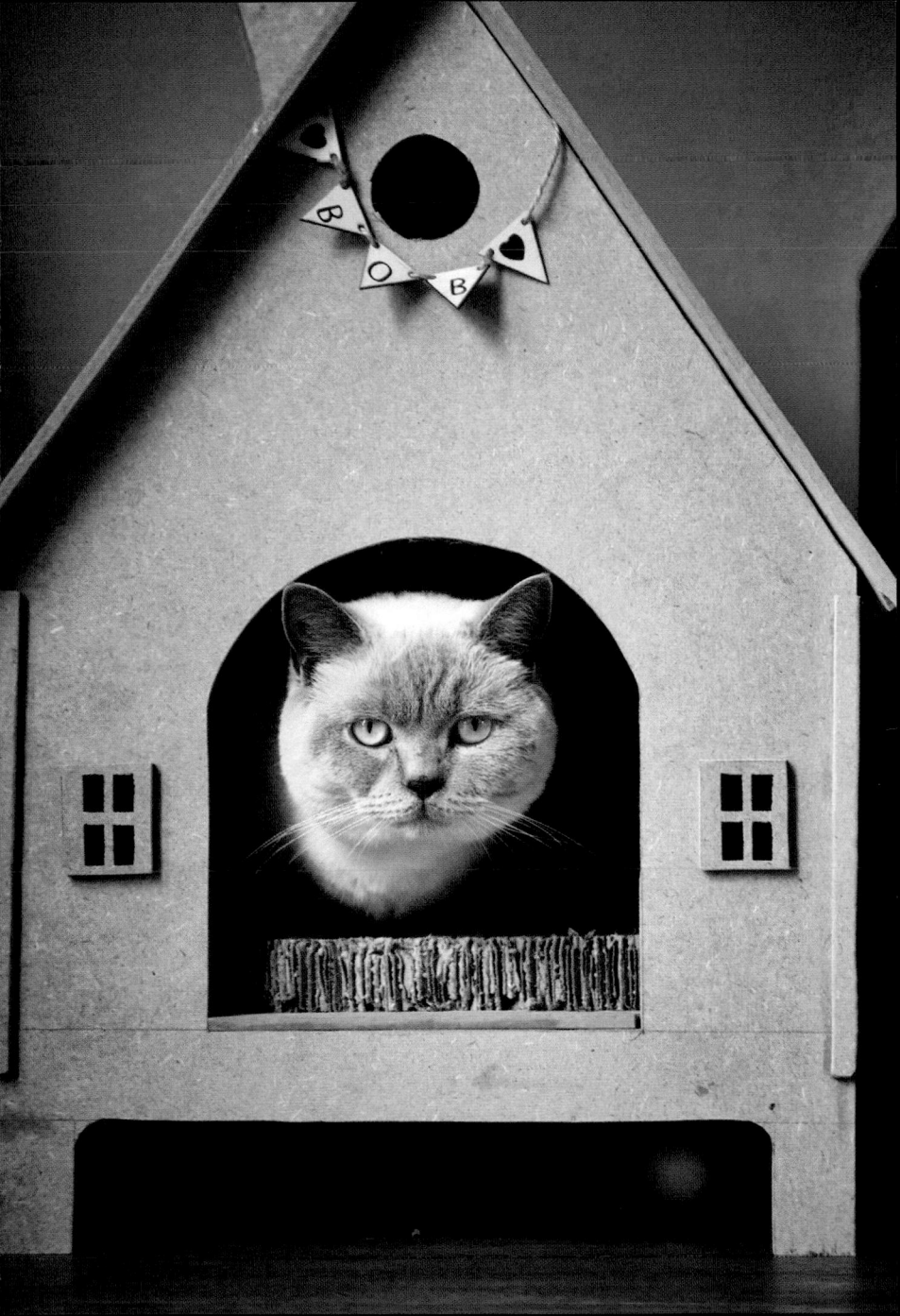
B
O
B

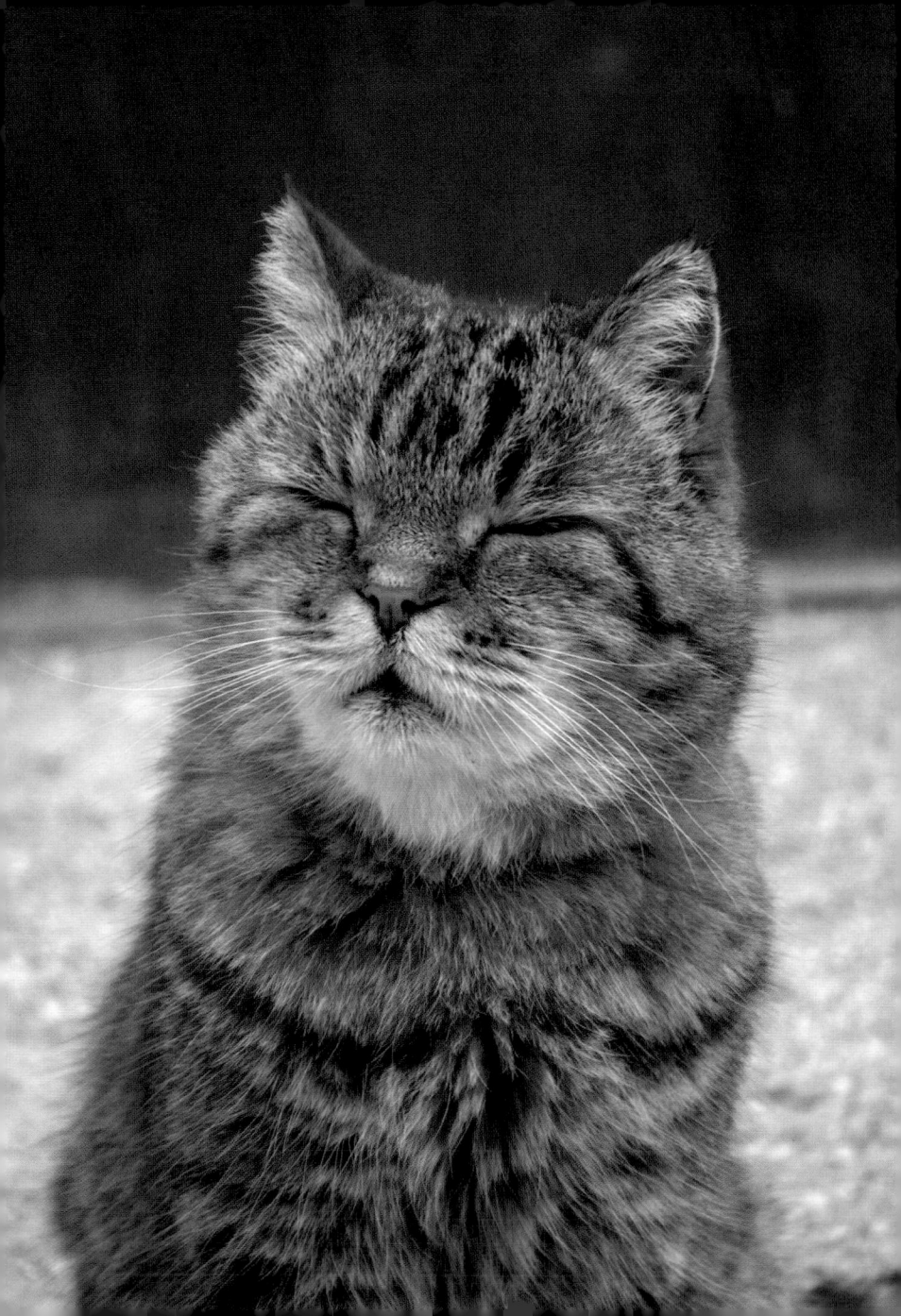

Go on then, bore me shitless about what you can do with an Excel spreadsheet

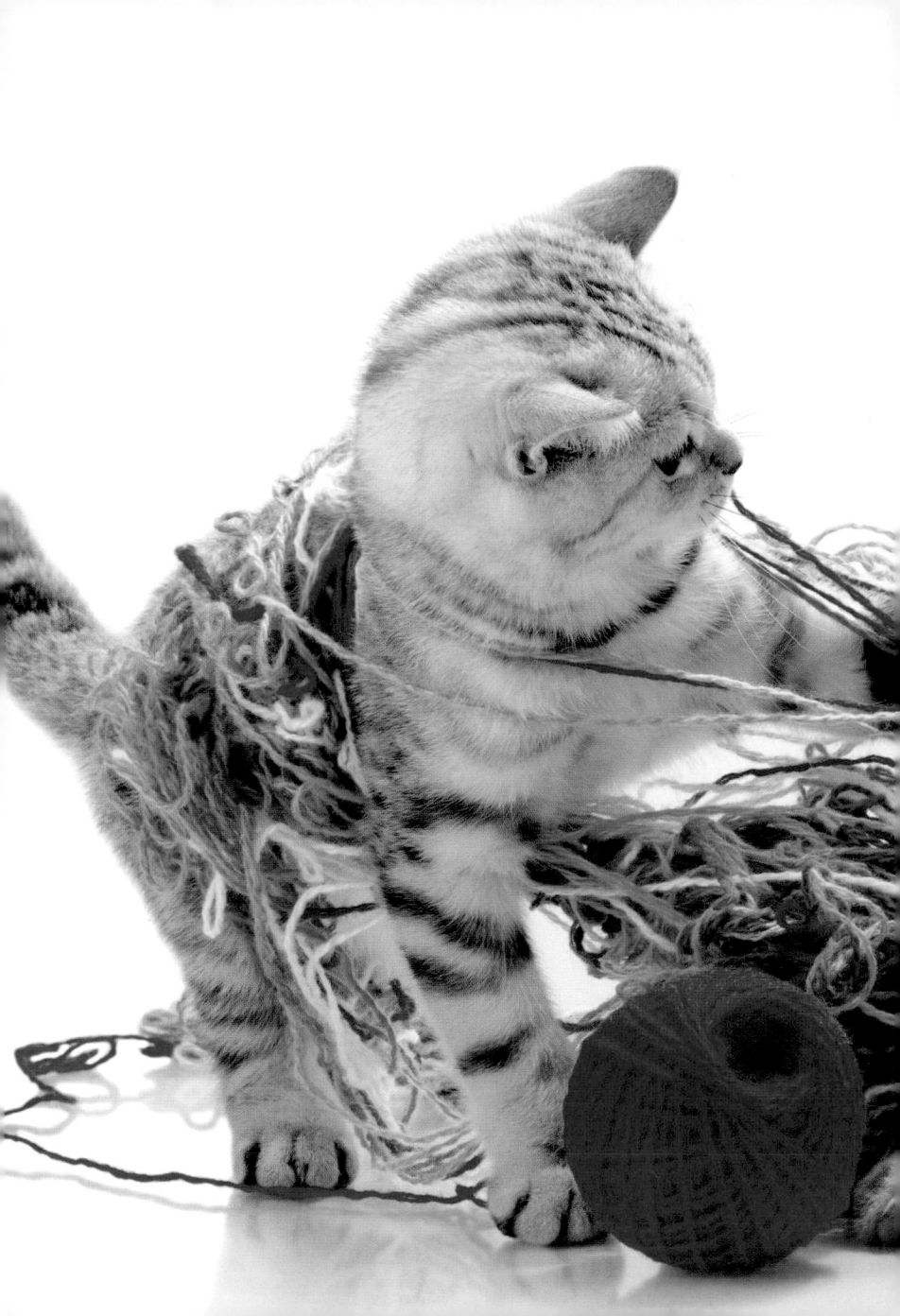

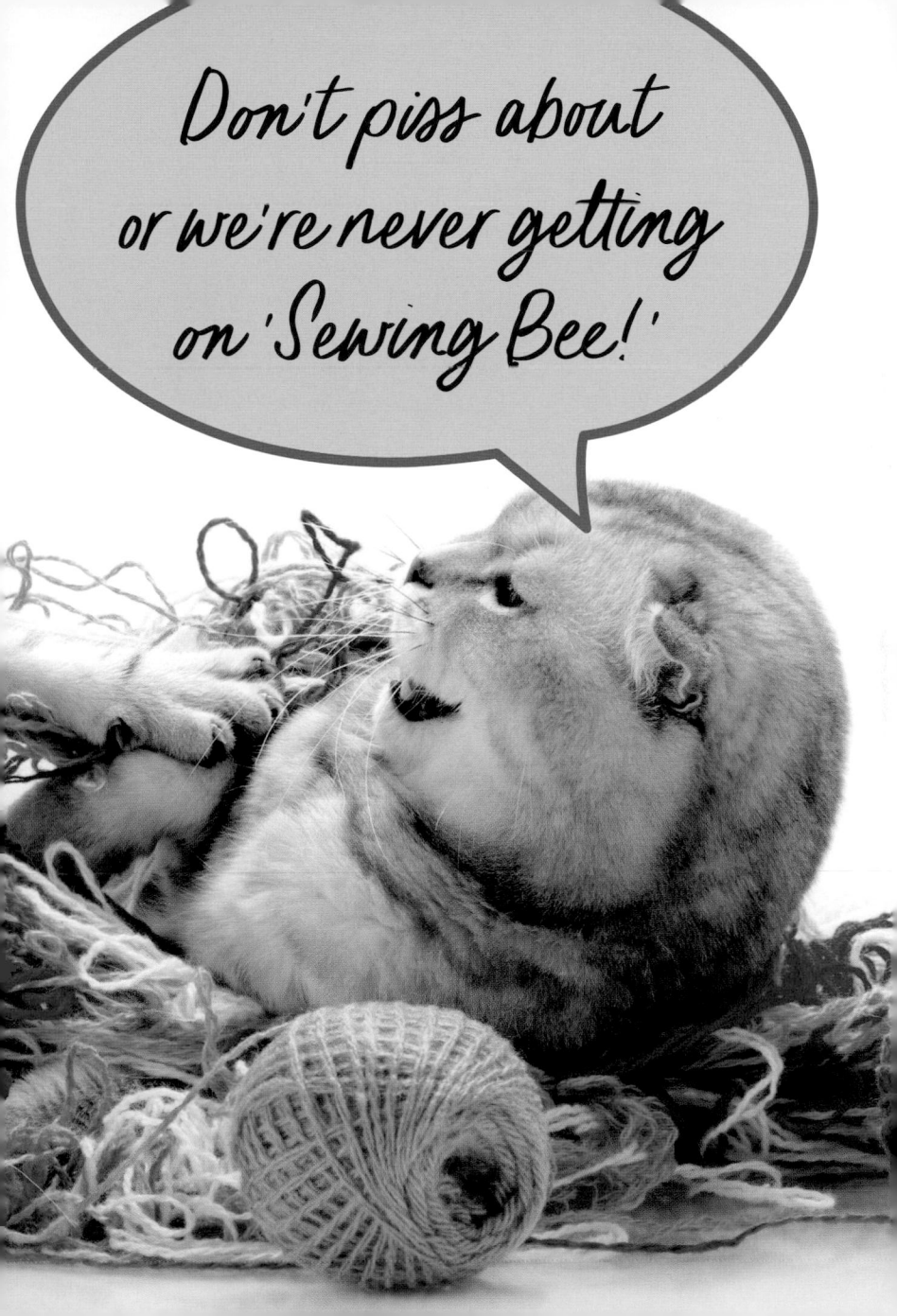
Don't piss about
or we're never getting
on 'Sewing Bee!'

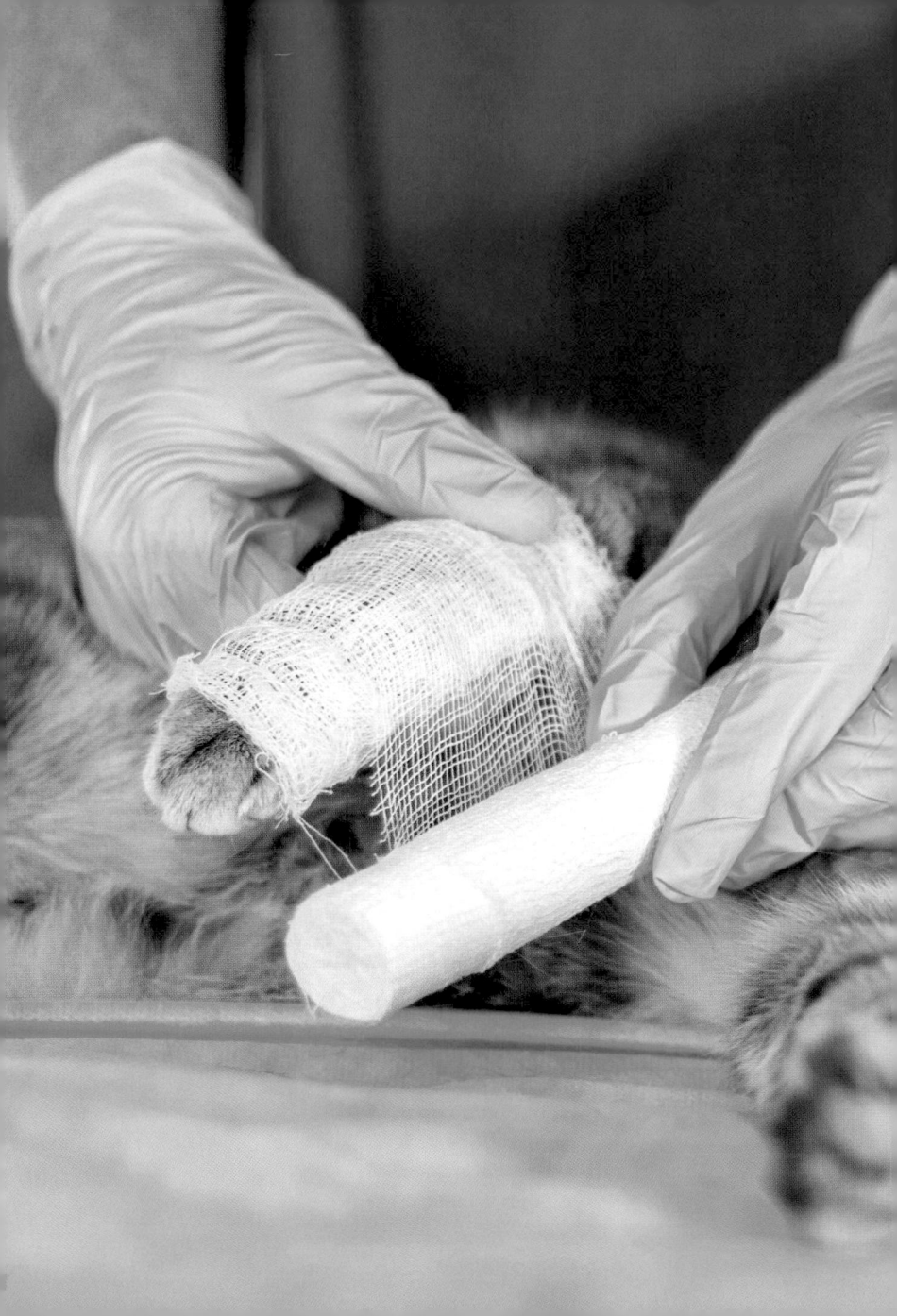

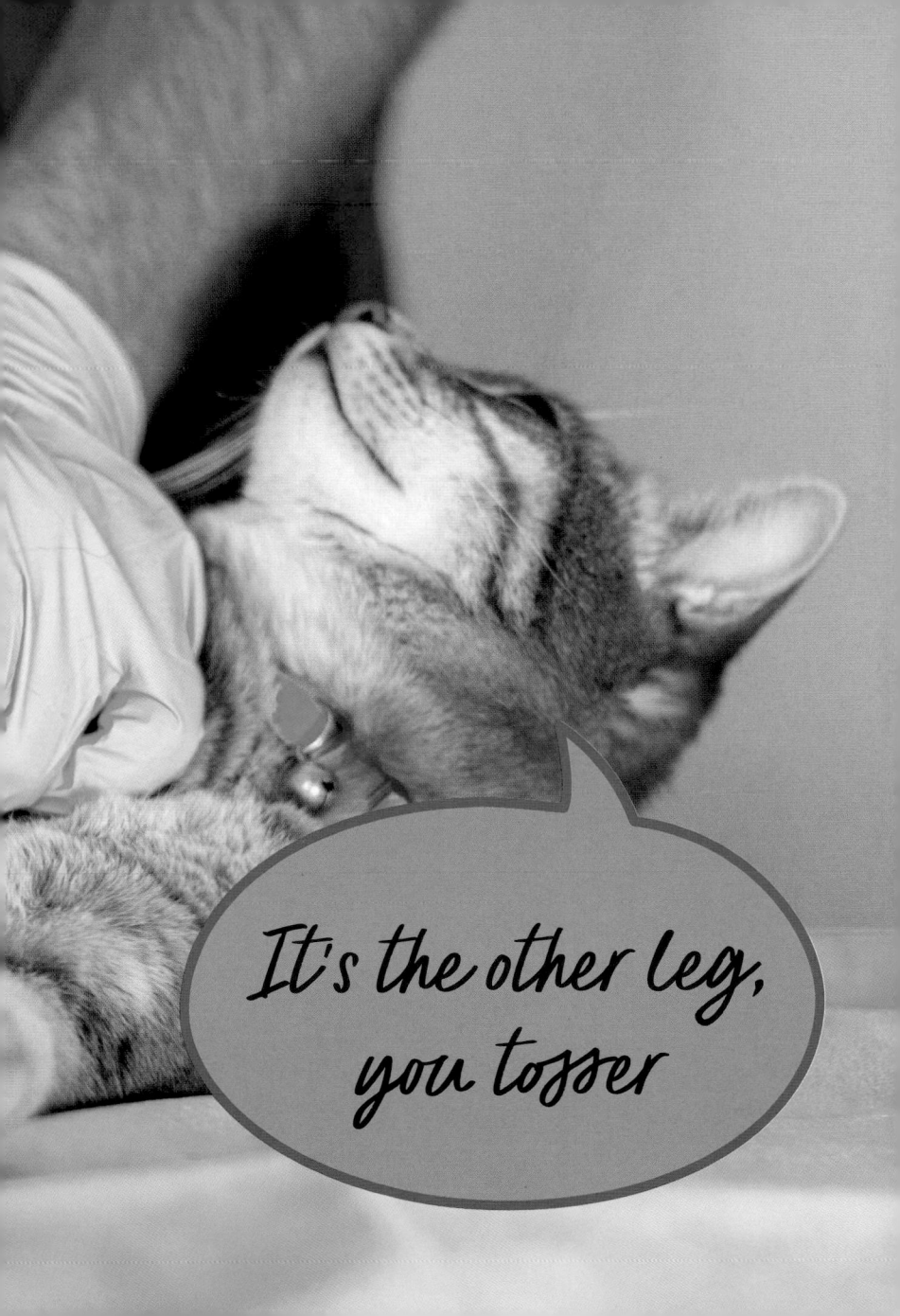
It's the other leg,
you tosser

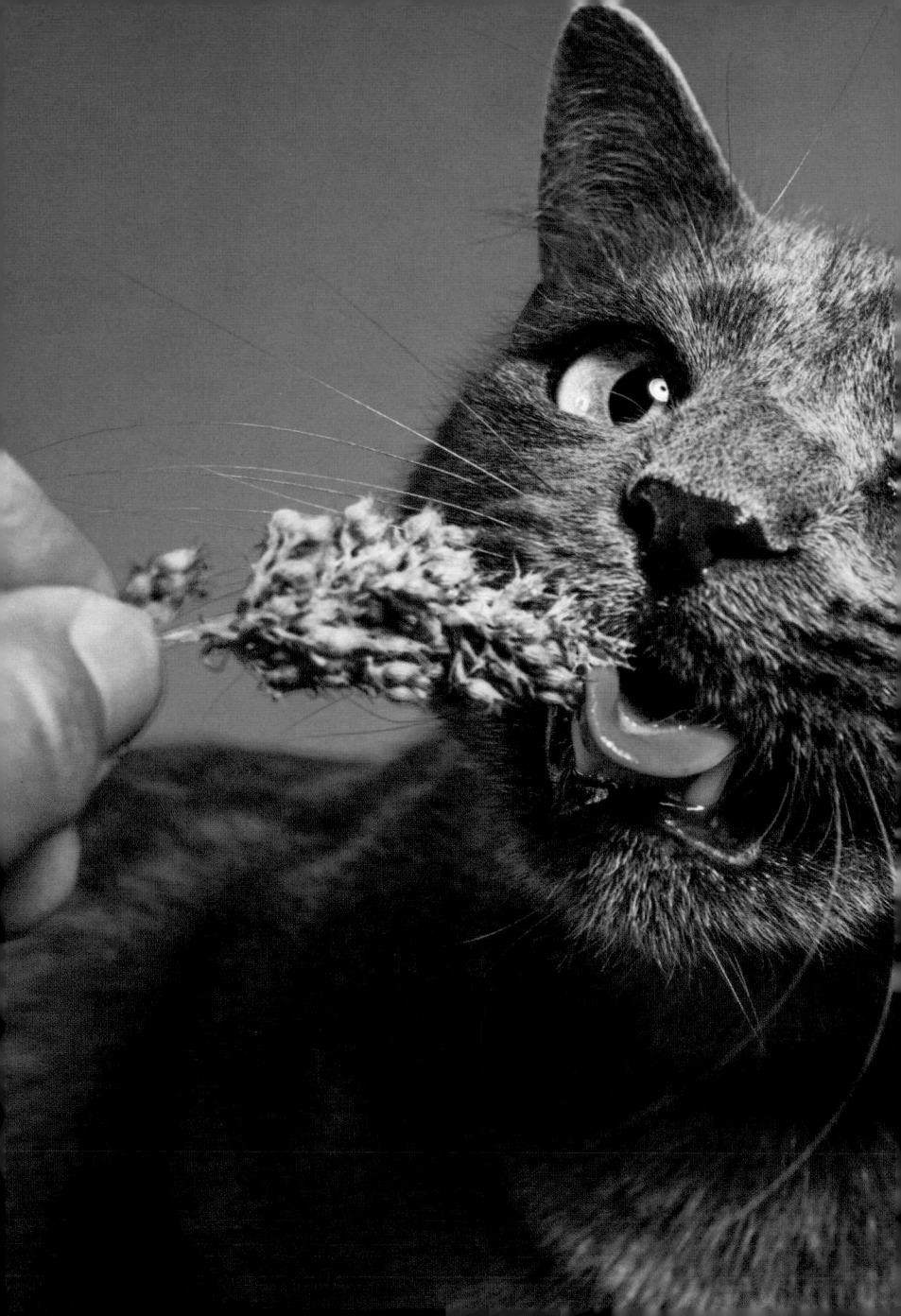

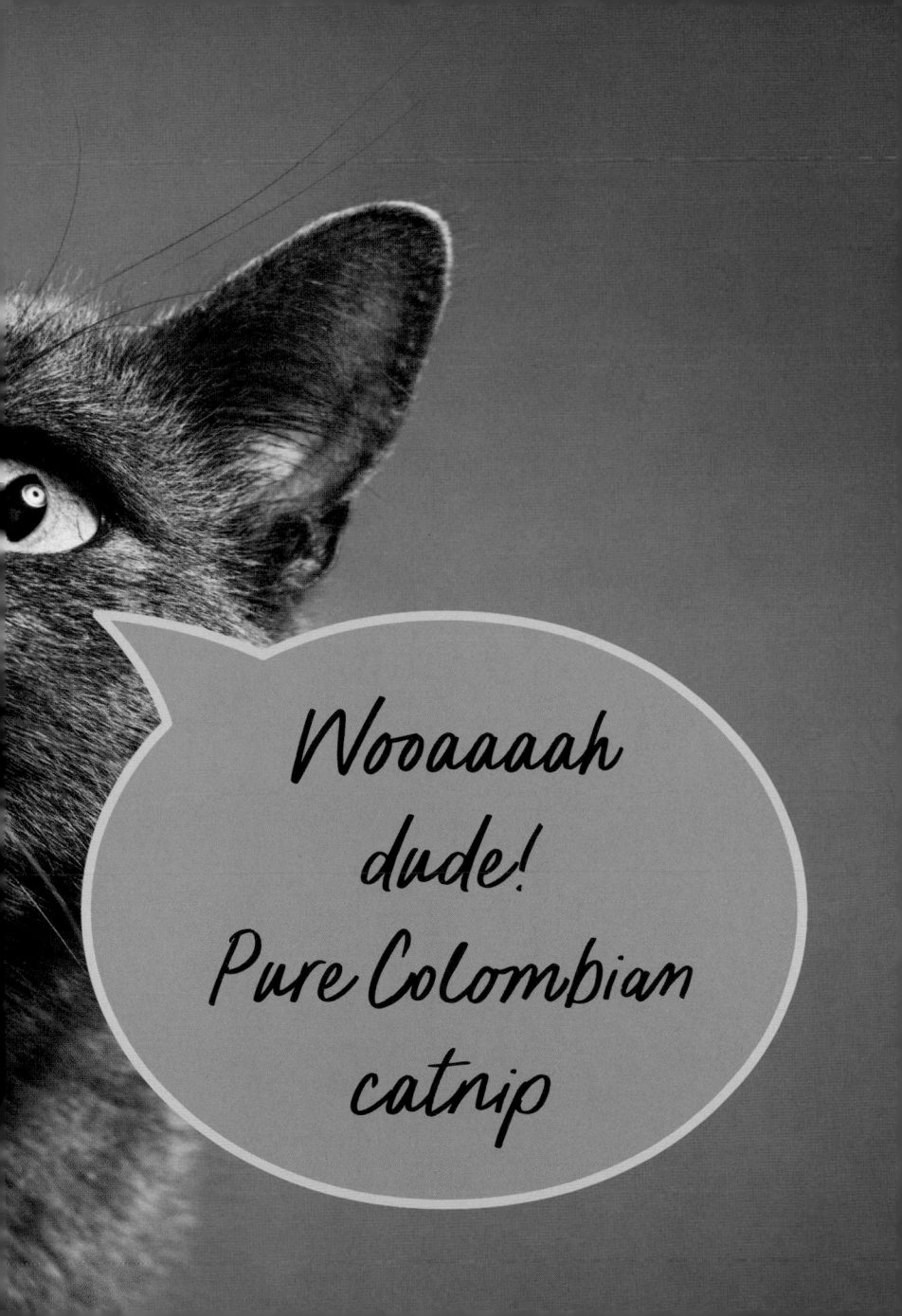
Wooaaaah
dude!
Pure Colombian
catnip

Yep, the trampoline still works

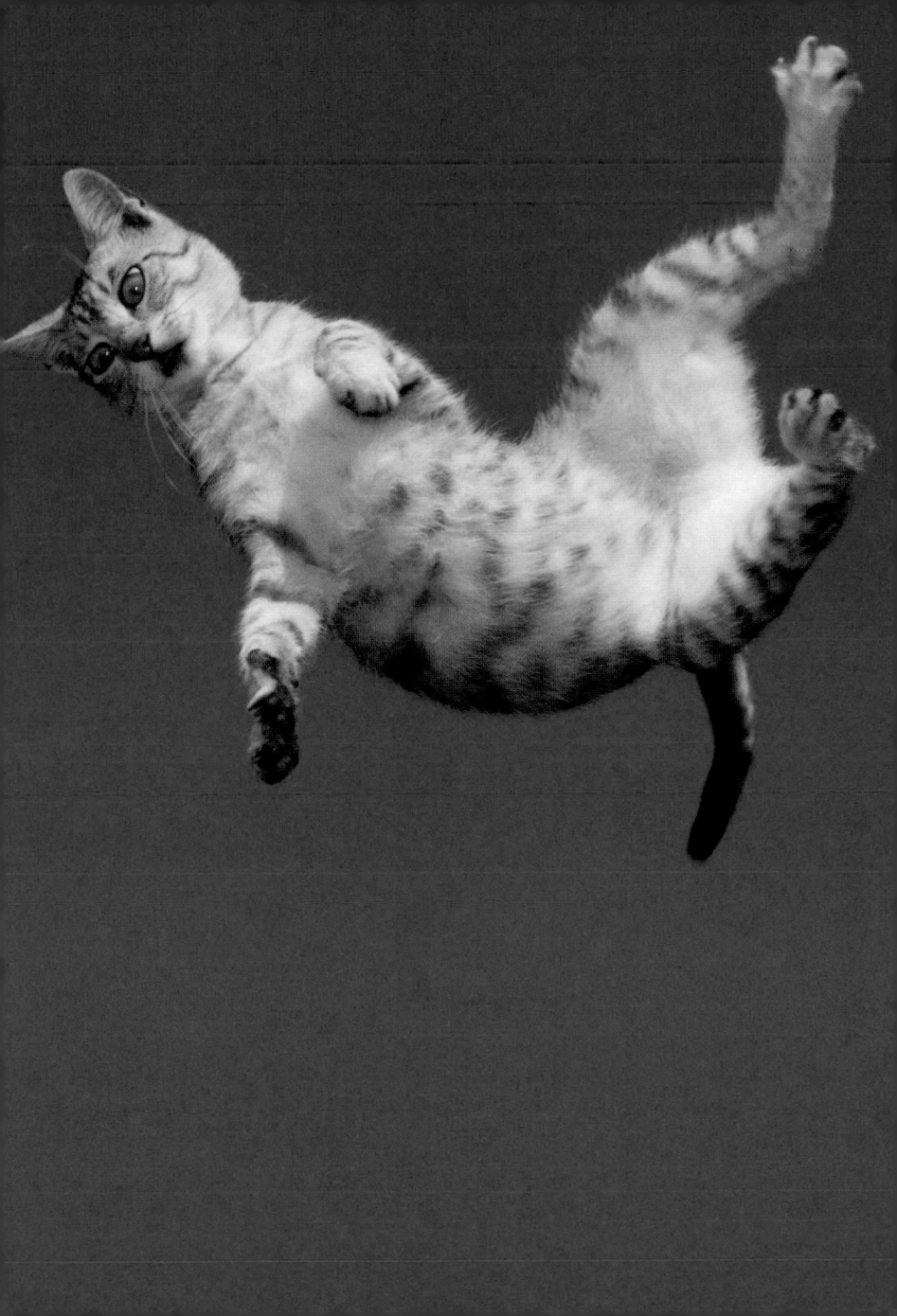

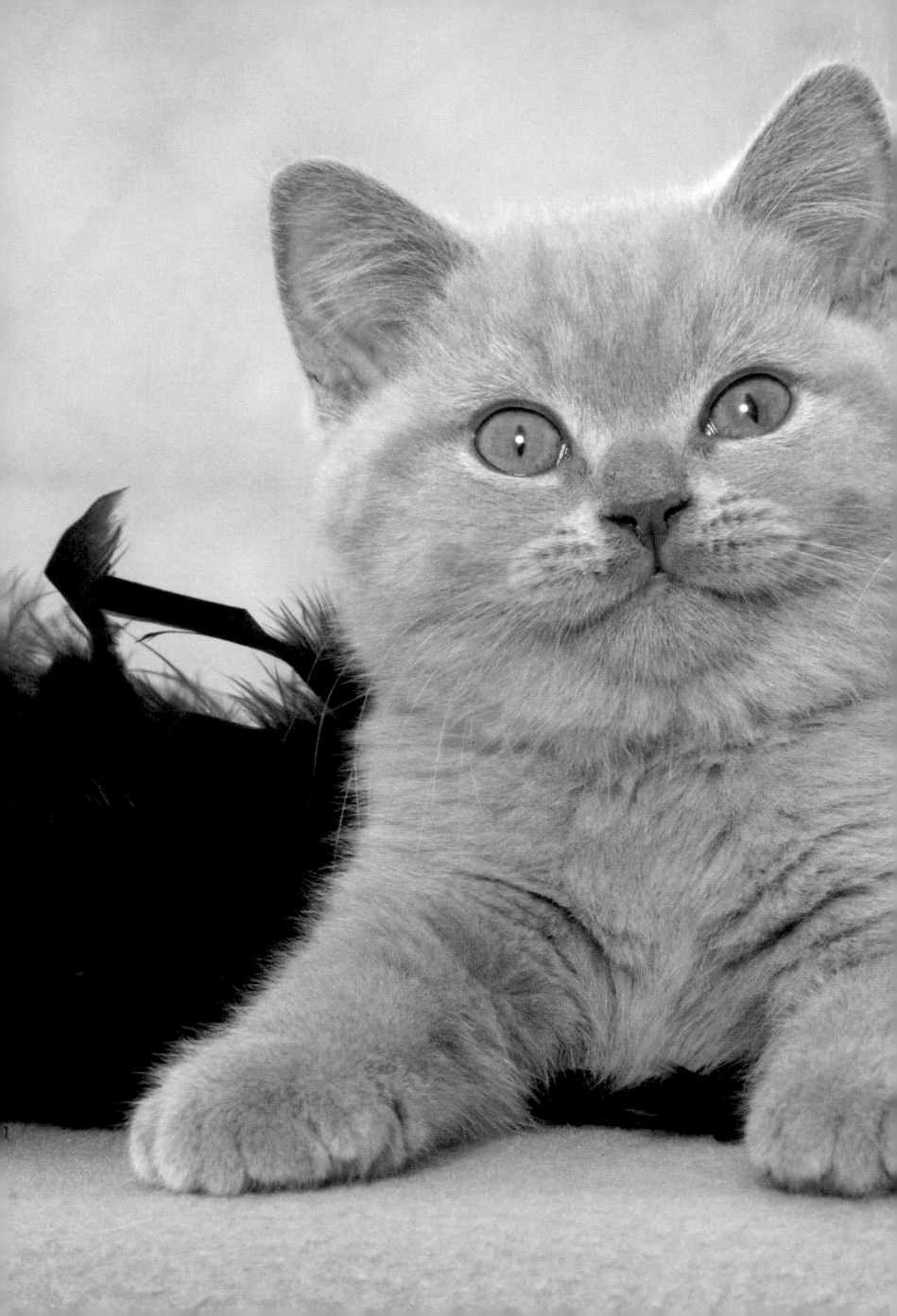

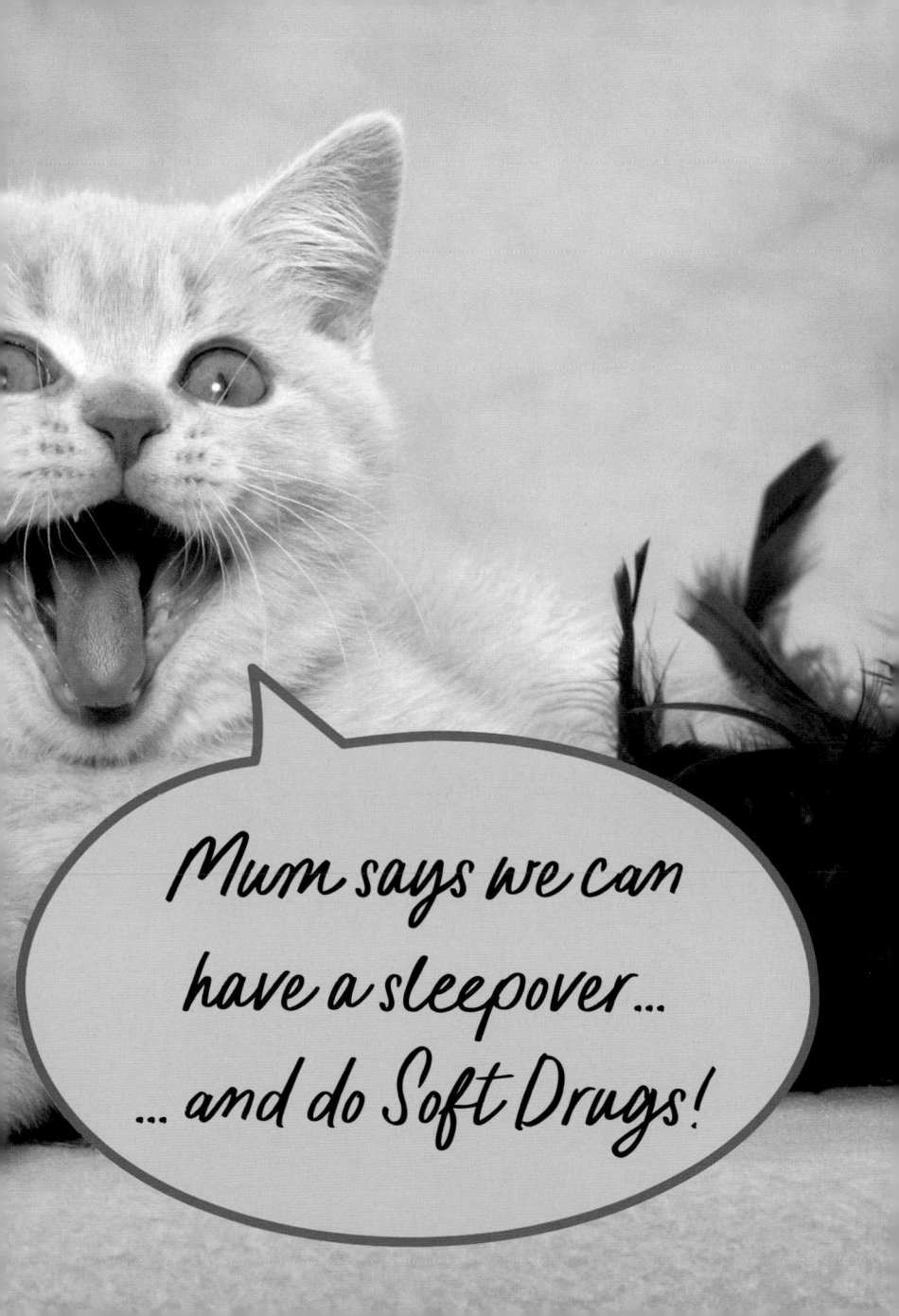
Mum says we can
have a sleepover...
... and do Soft Drugs!

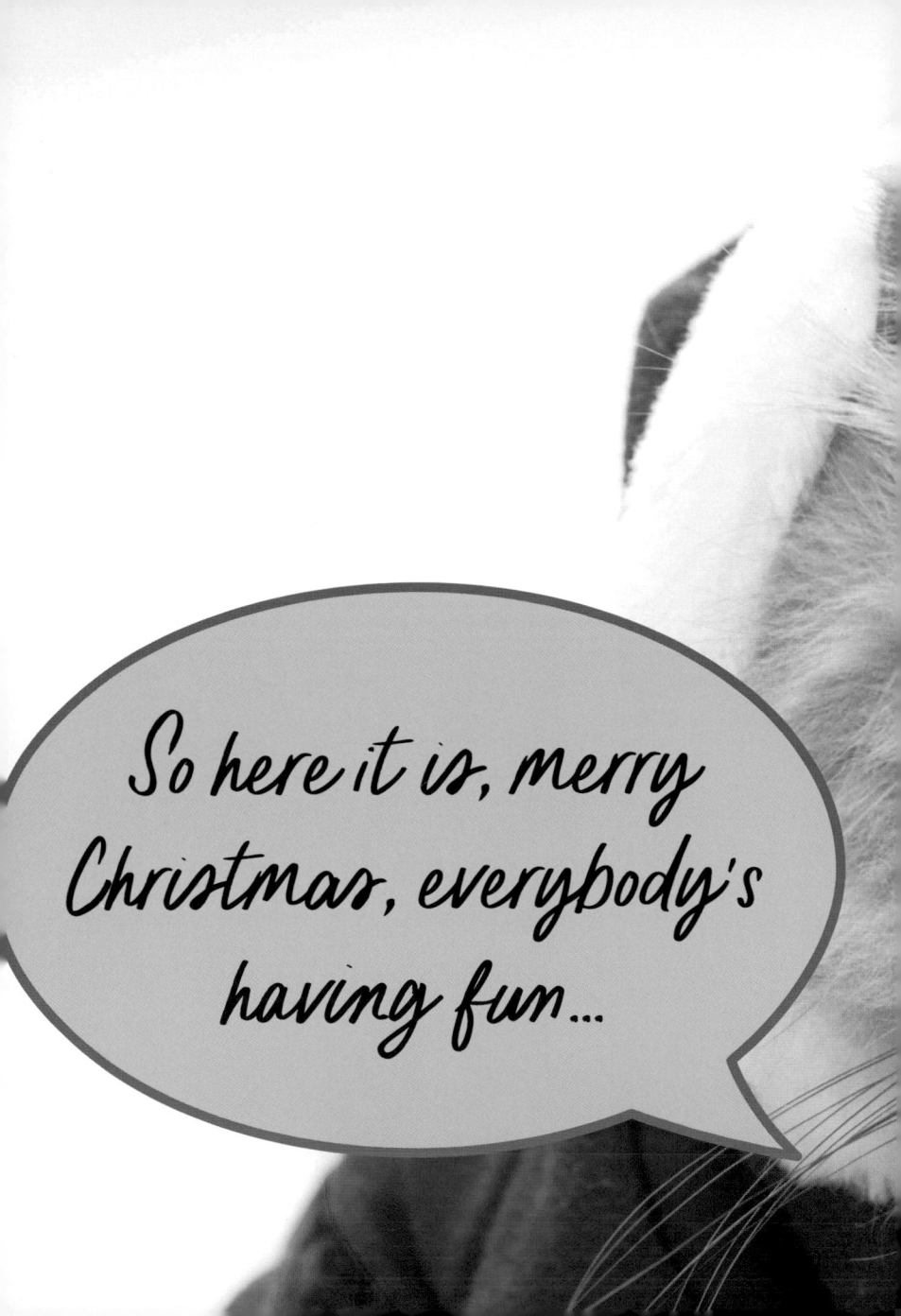
So here it is, merry
Christmas, everybody's
having fun...

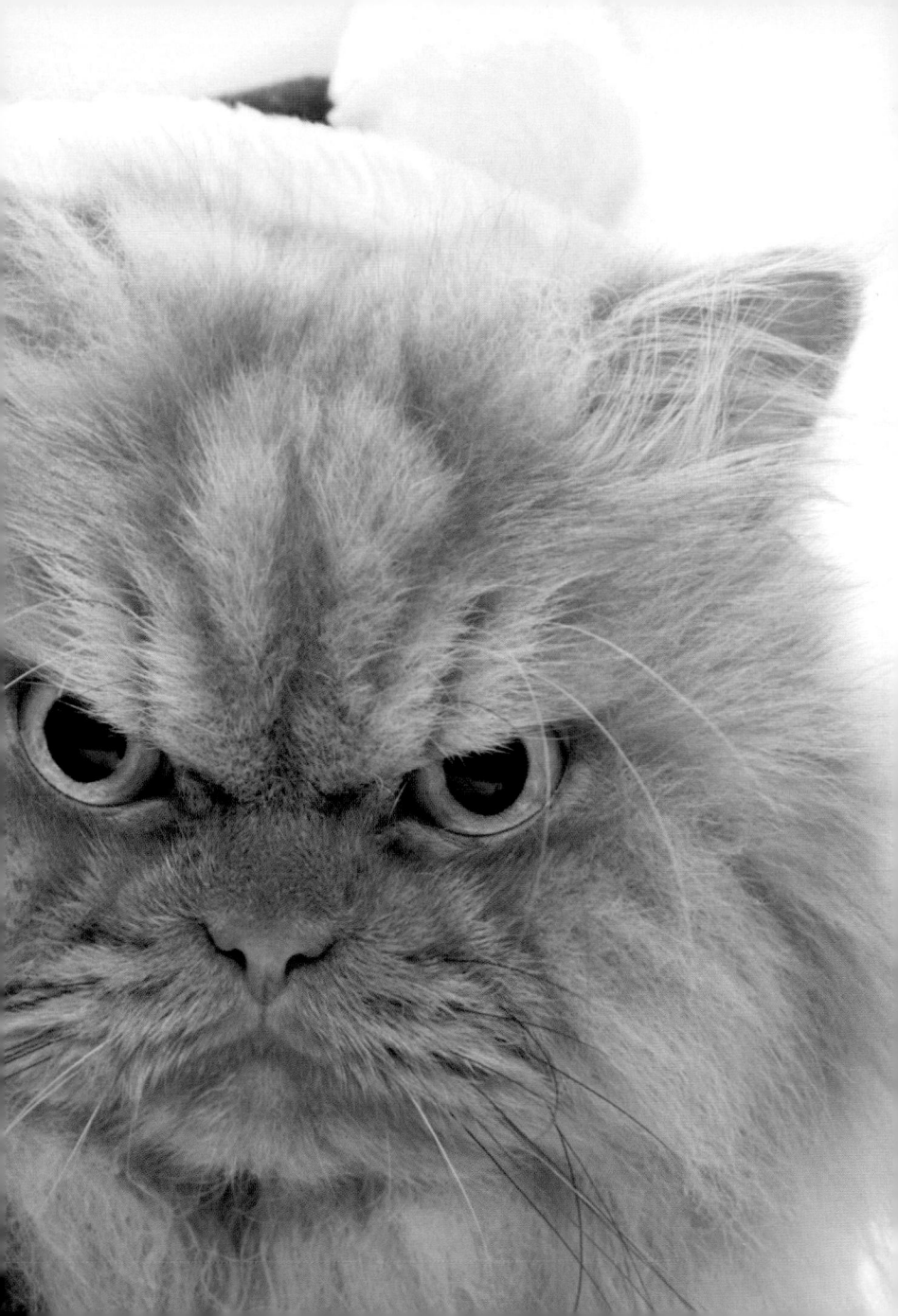

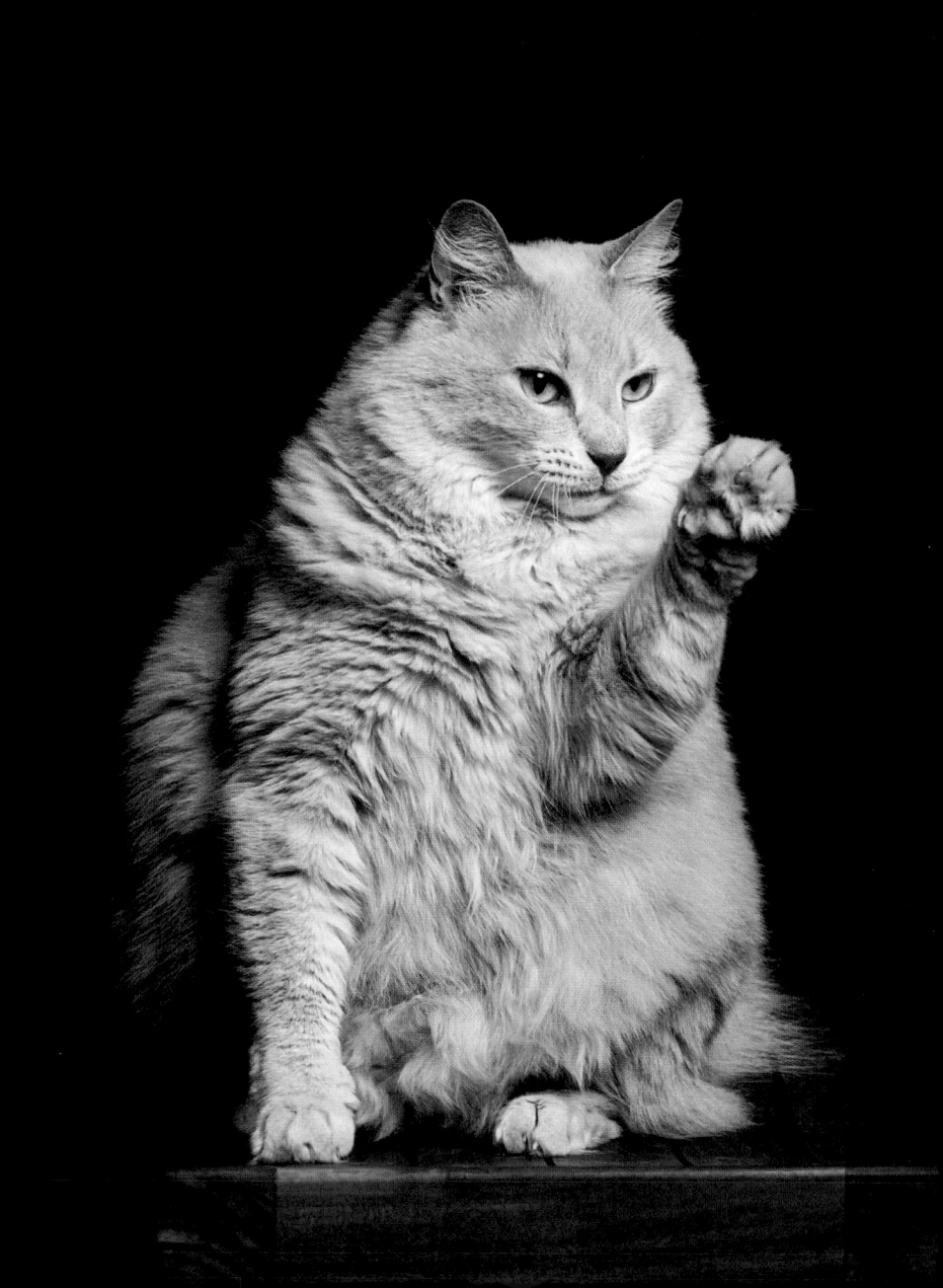

I AM THE CONDUCTOR! And when I point at you, First Violin, I don't expect you to be licking your fucking arse!

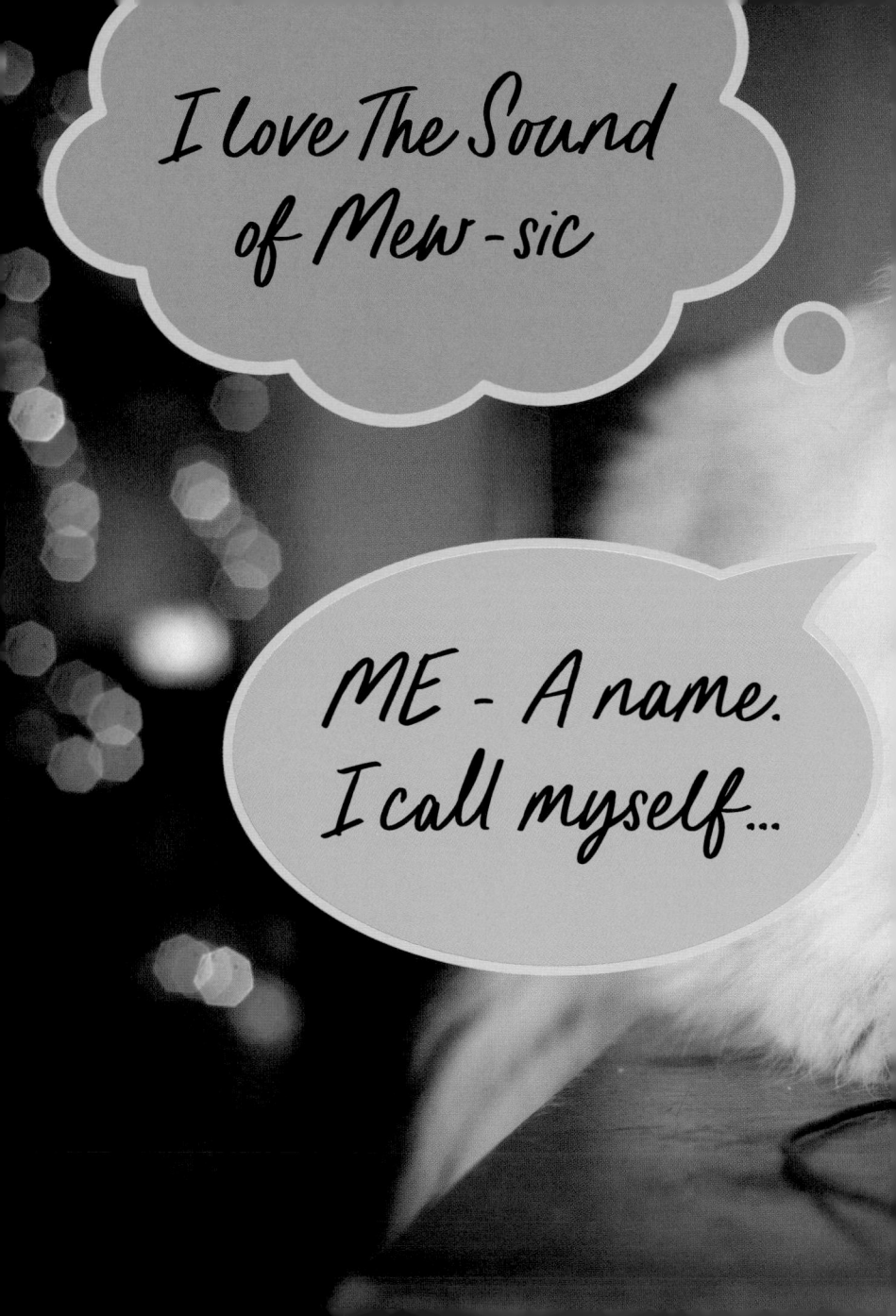
I love The Sound of Mew-sic
ME - A name. I call myself...

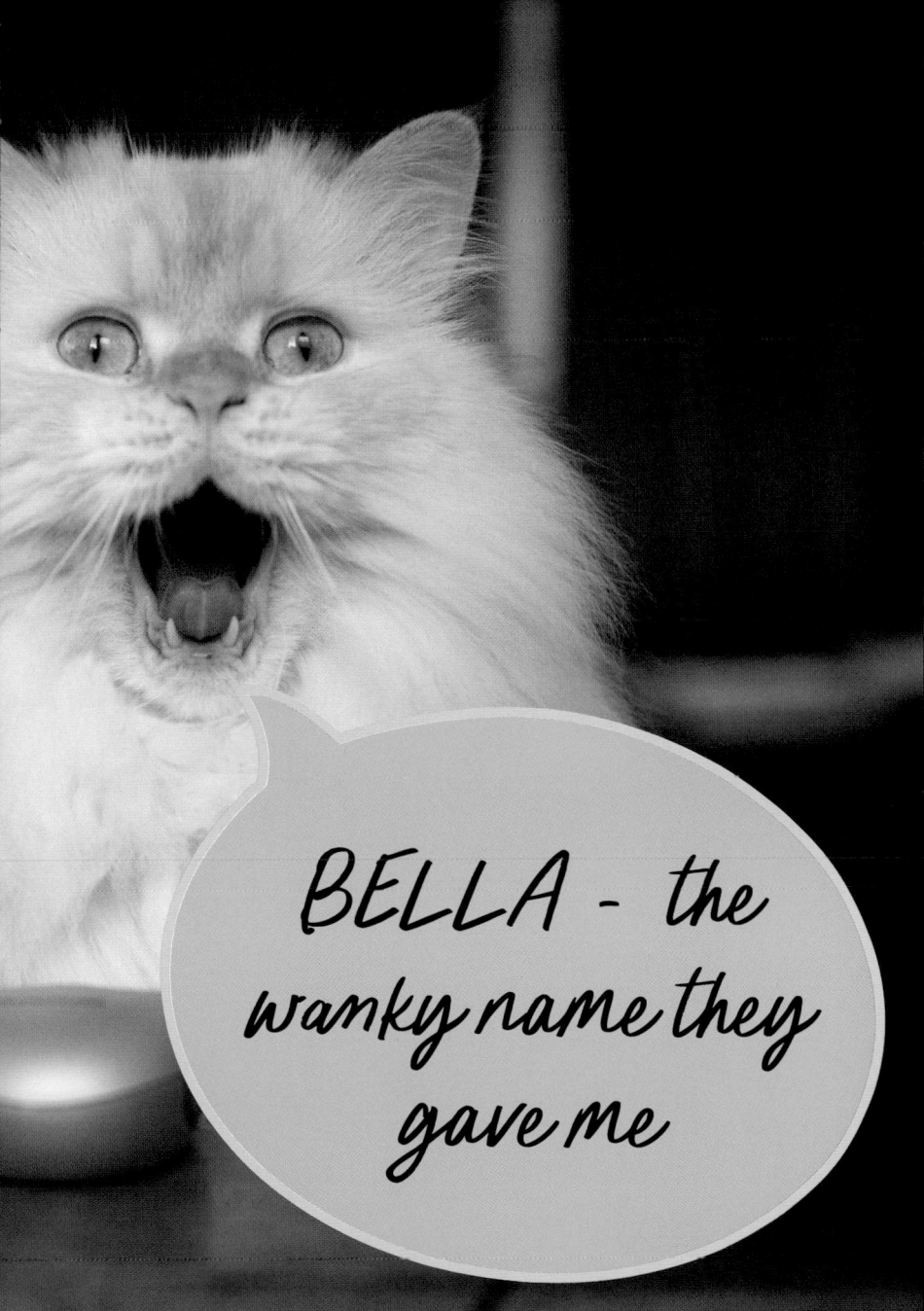
BELLA - the
wanky name they
gave me

FUCK OFF!
You noisy
scrounging
bastards!

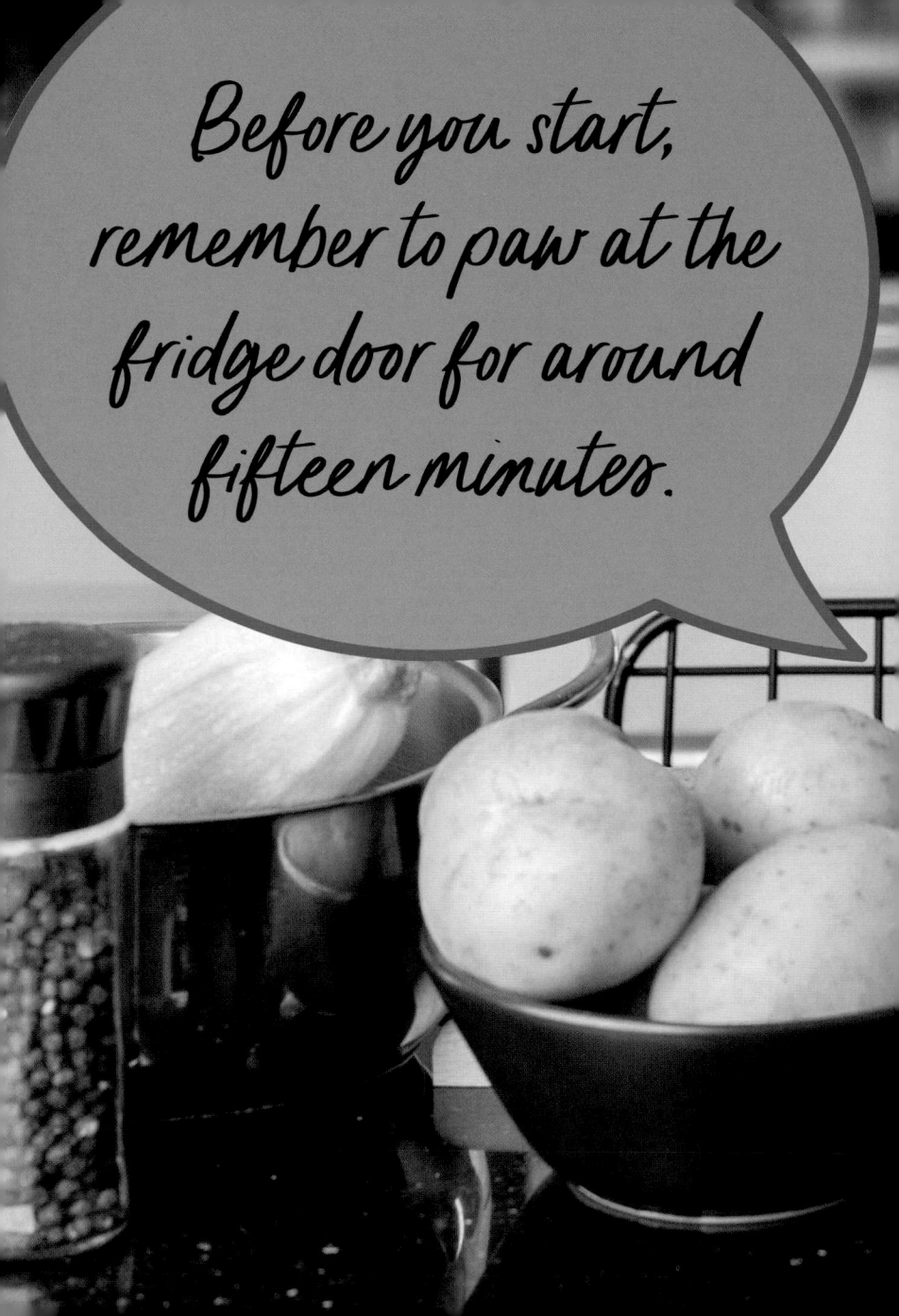
Before you start, remember to paw at the fridge door for around fifteen minutes.

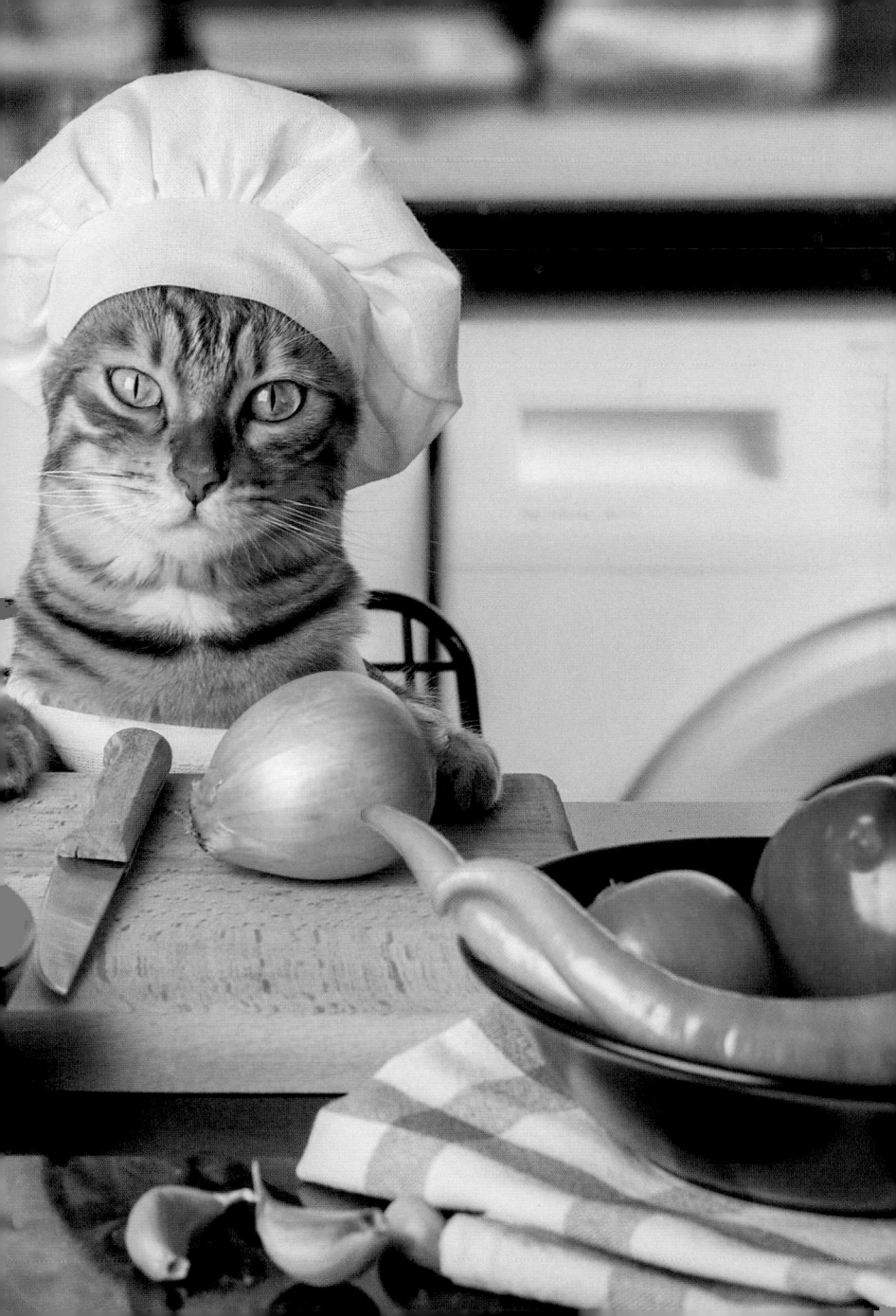

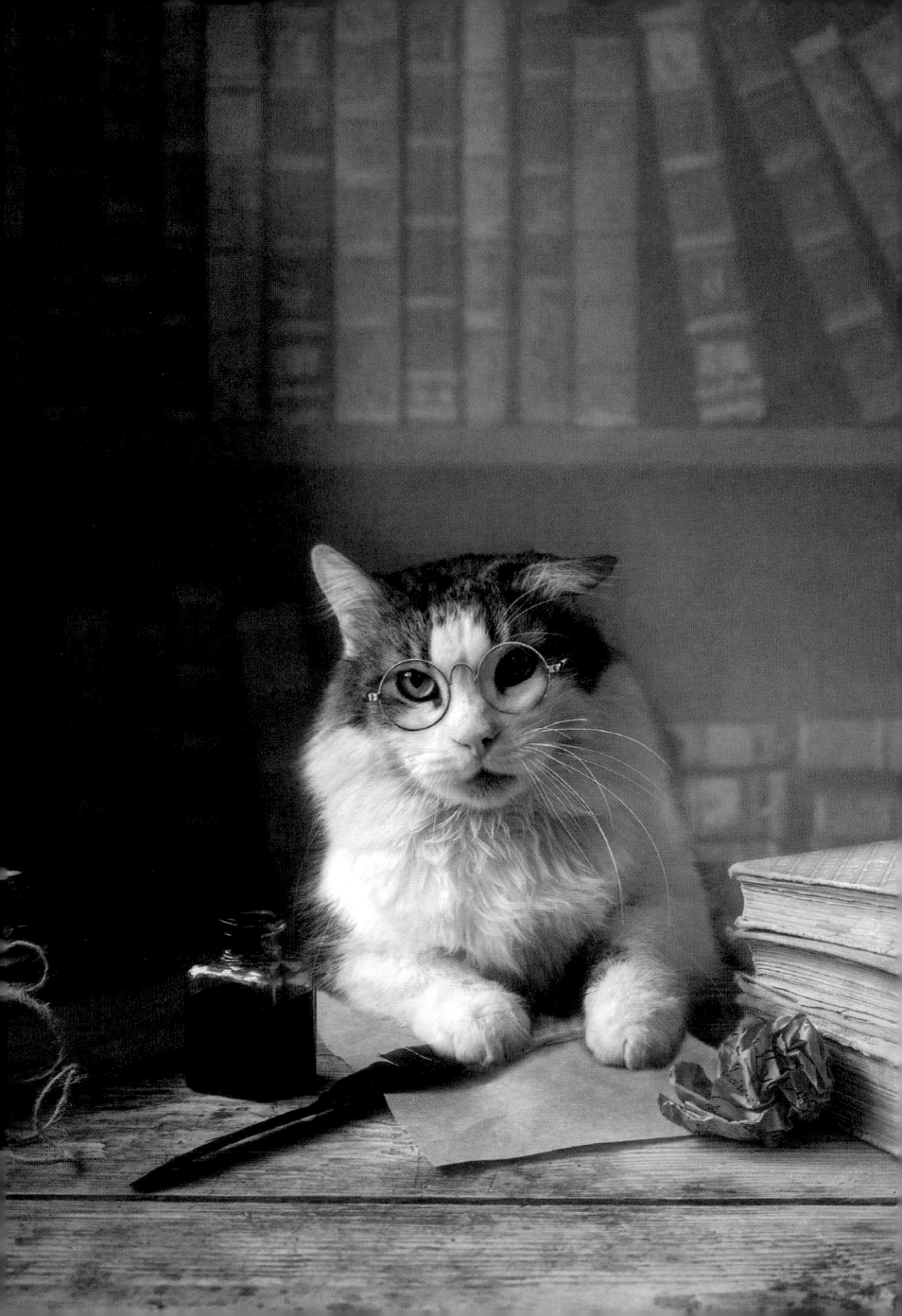

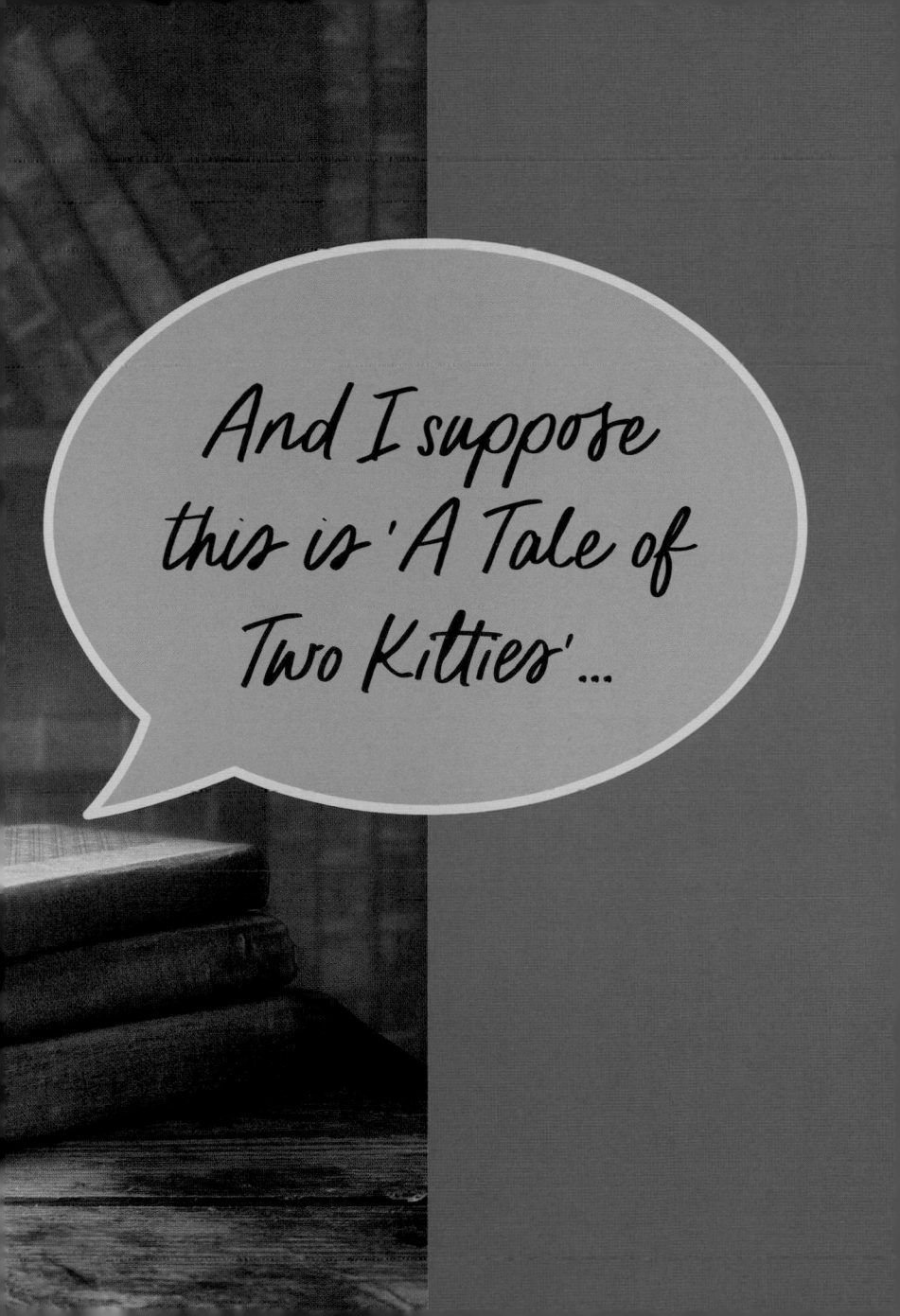
And I suppose this is 'A Tale of Two Kitties'...

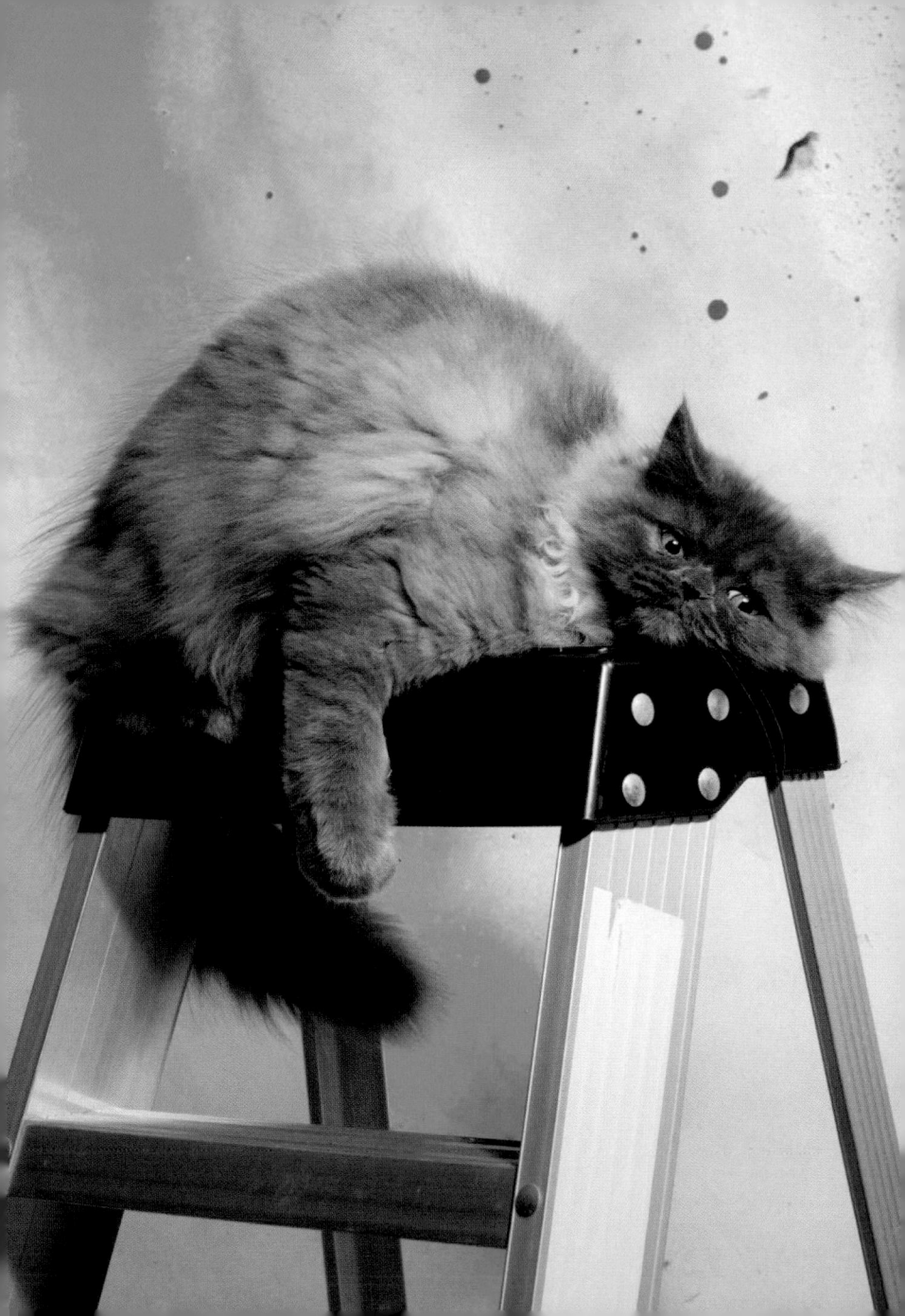

Fuck me, lying down's hard work

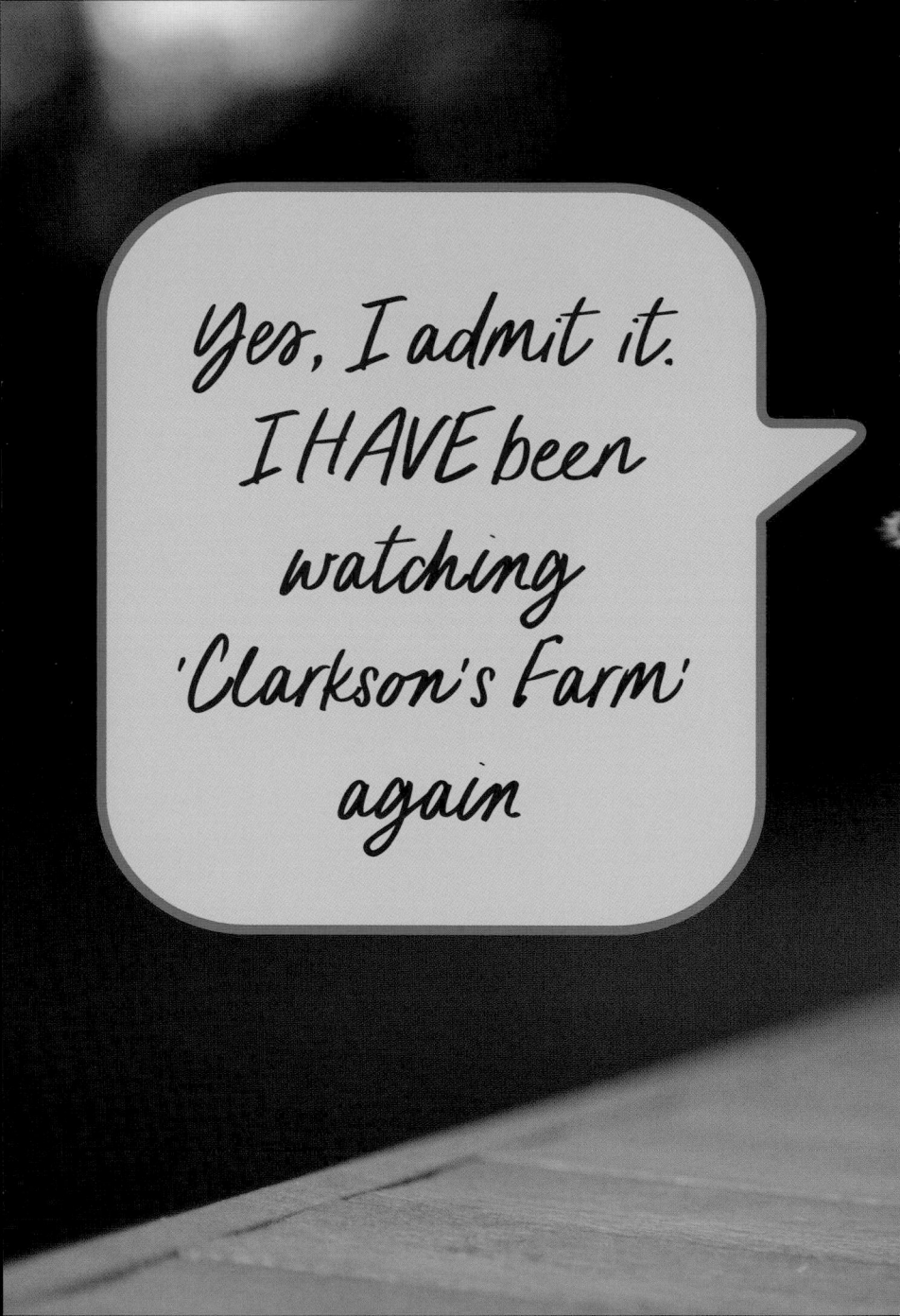
Yes, I admit it.
I HAVE been
watching
'Clarkson's Farm'
again

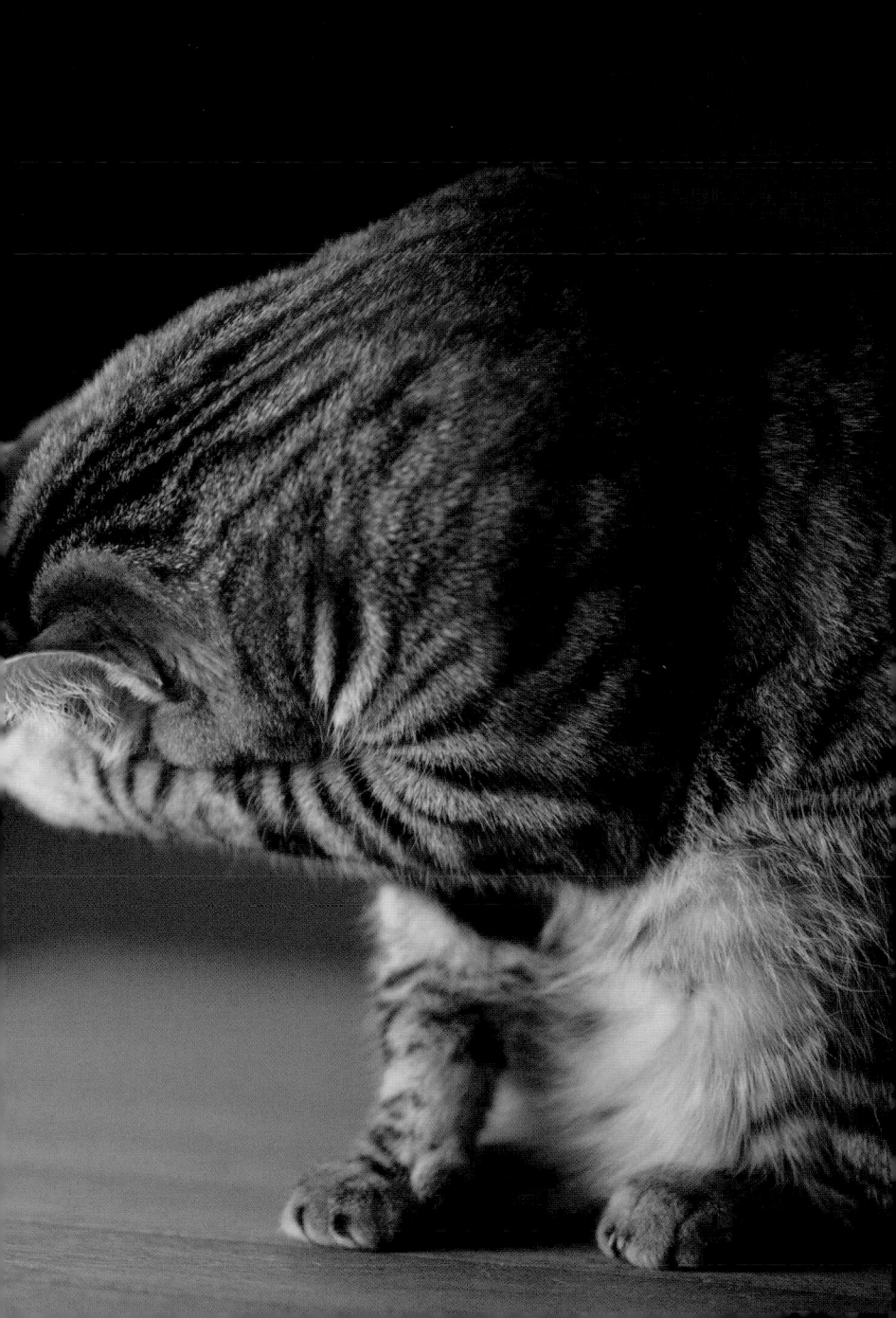

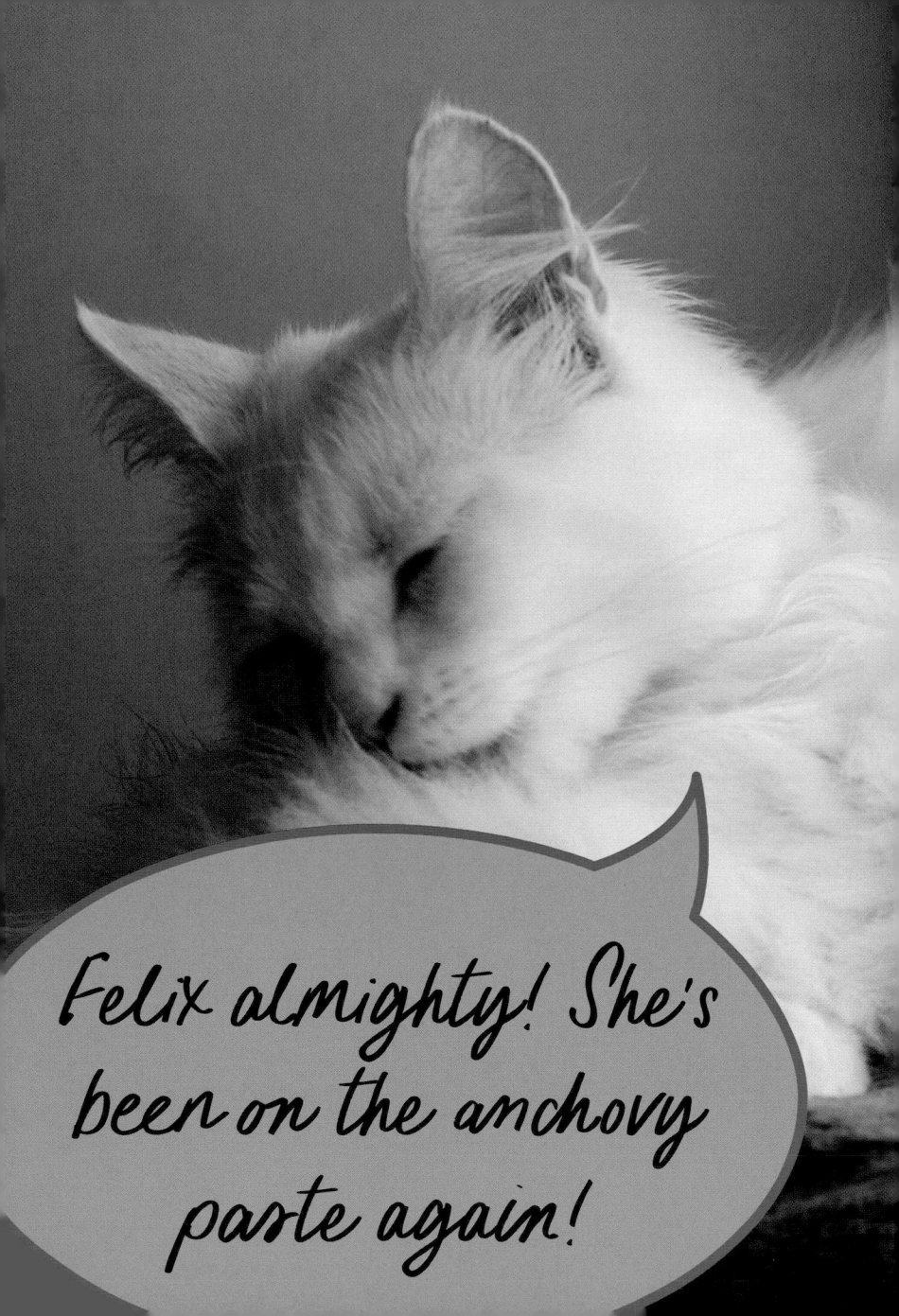
Felix almighty! She's
been on the anchovy
paste again!

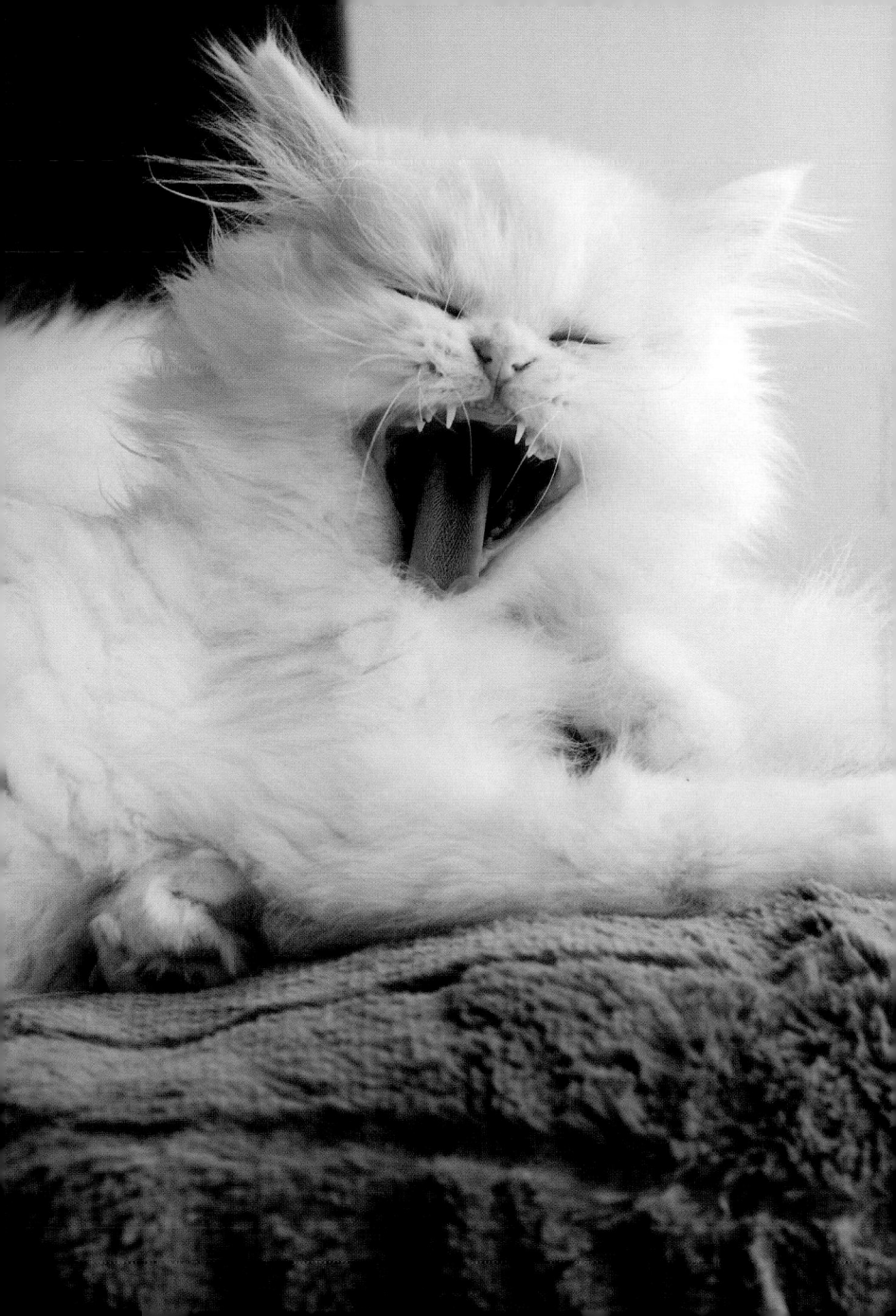

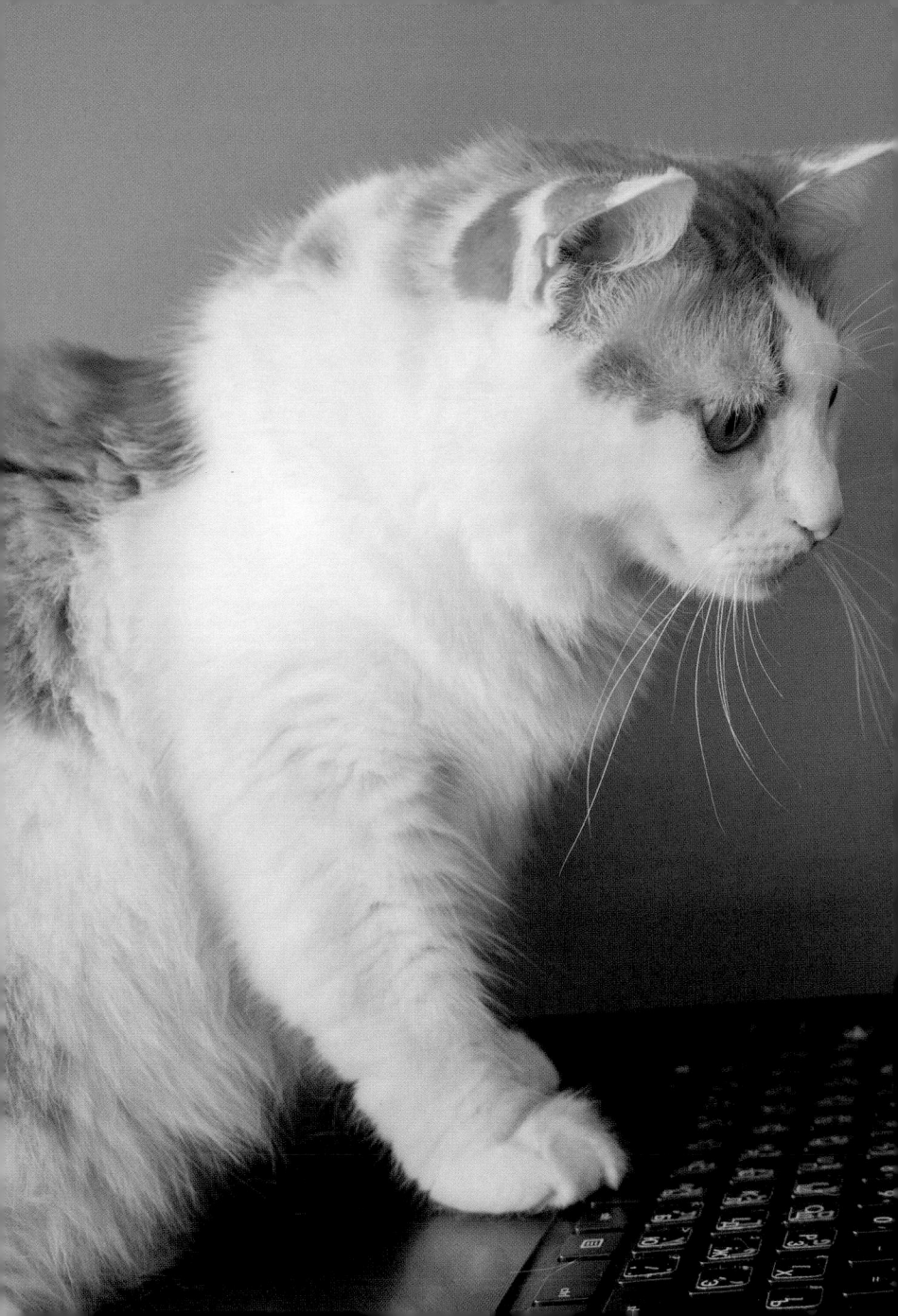

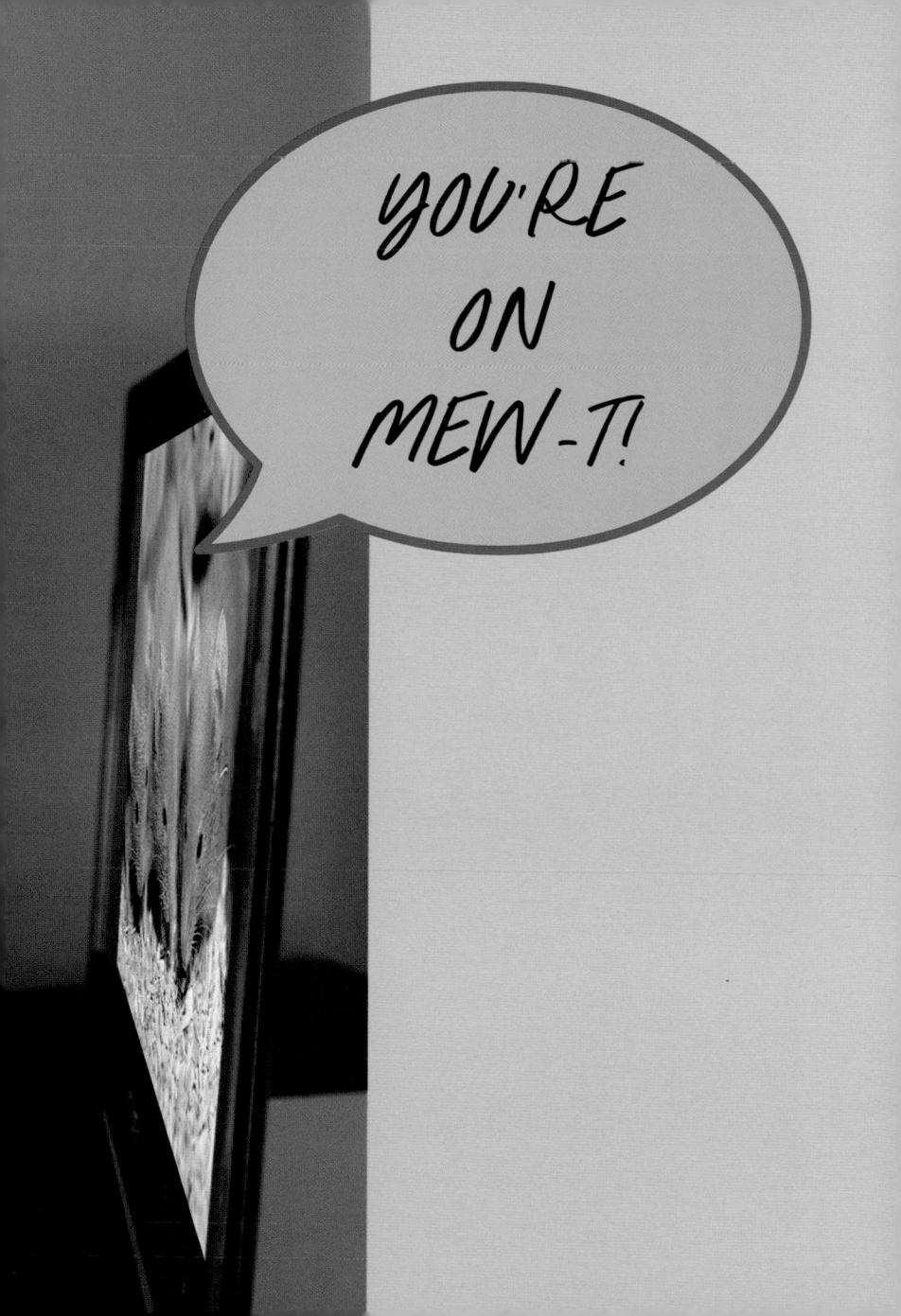
YOU'RE
ON
MEW-T!

Hey, I love mime workshops. I'm steering a car! I'm steering a car!

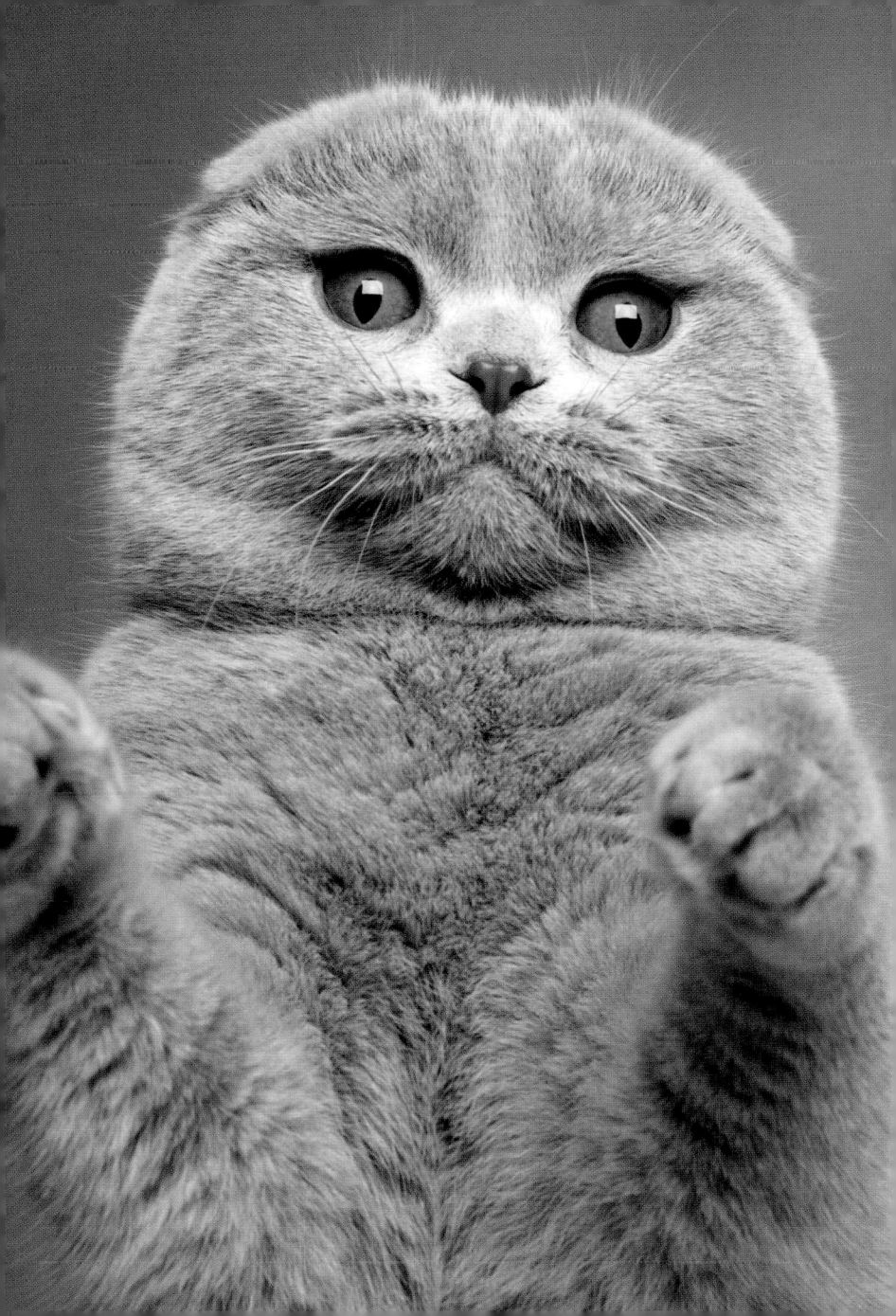

Oh no, stop it! Babe, you fucking crack me up!

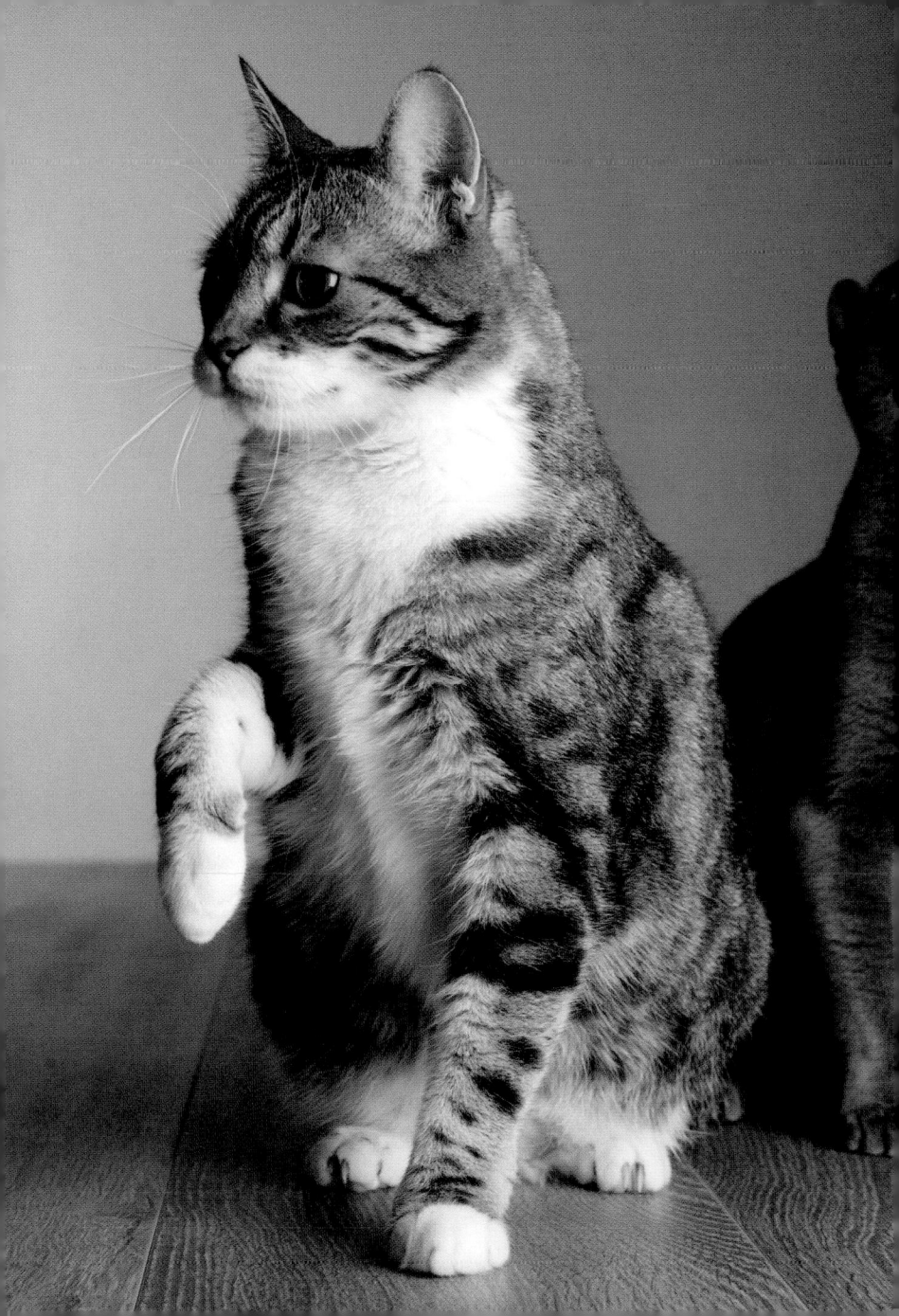

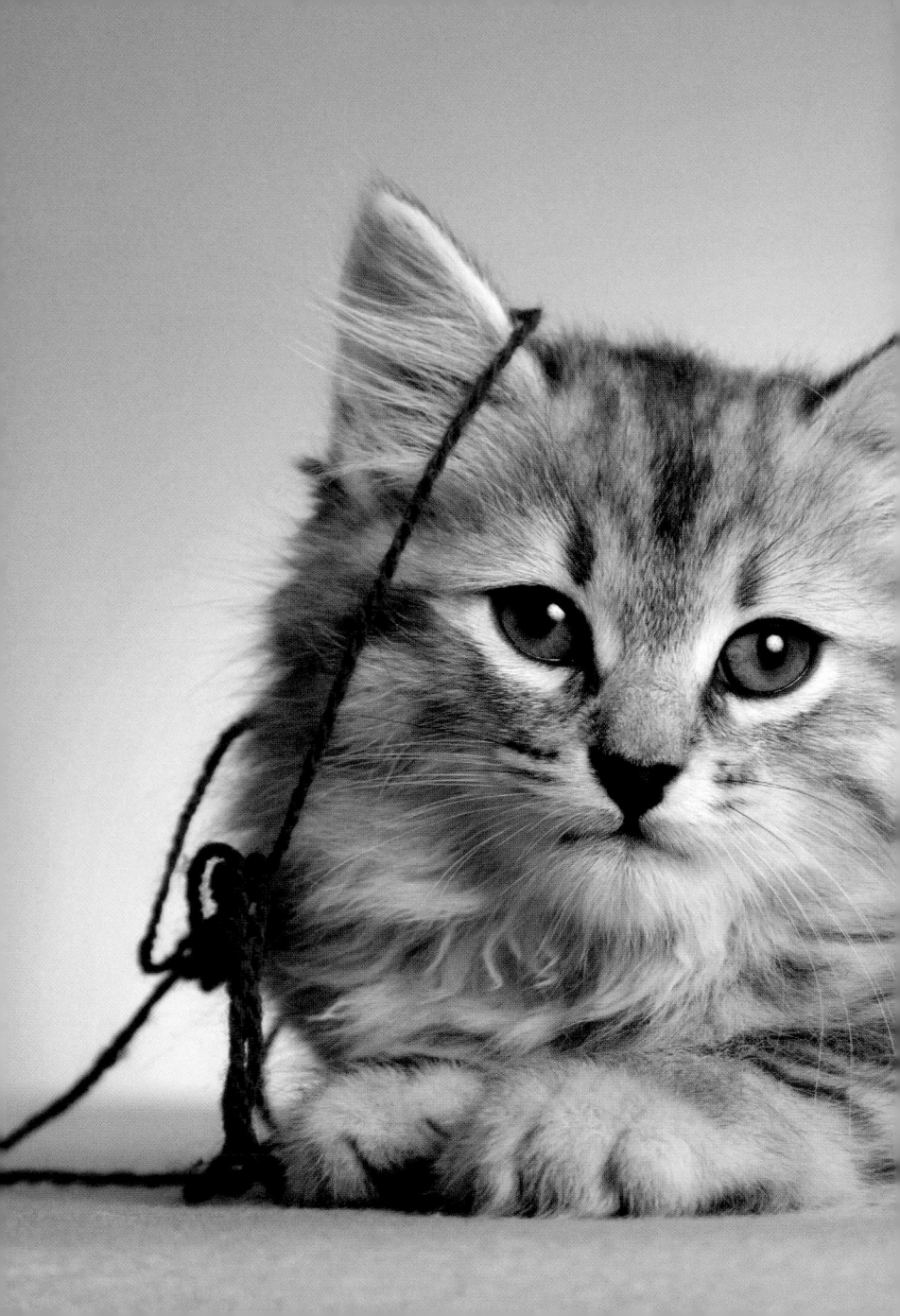

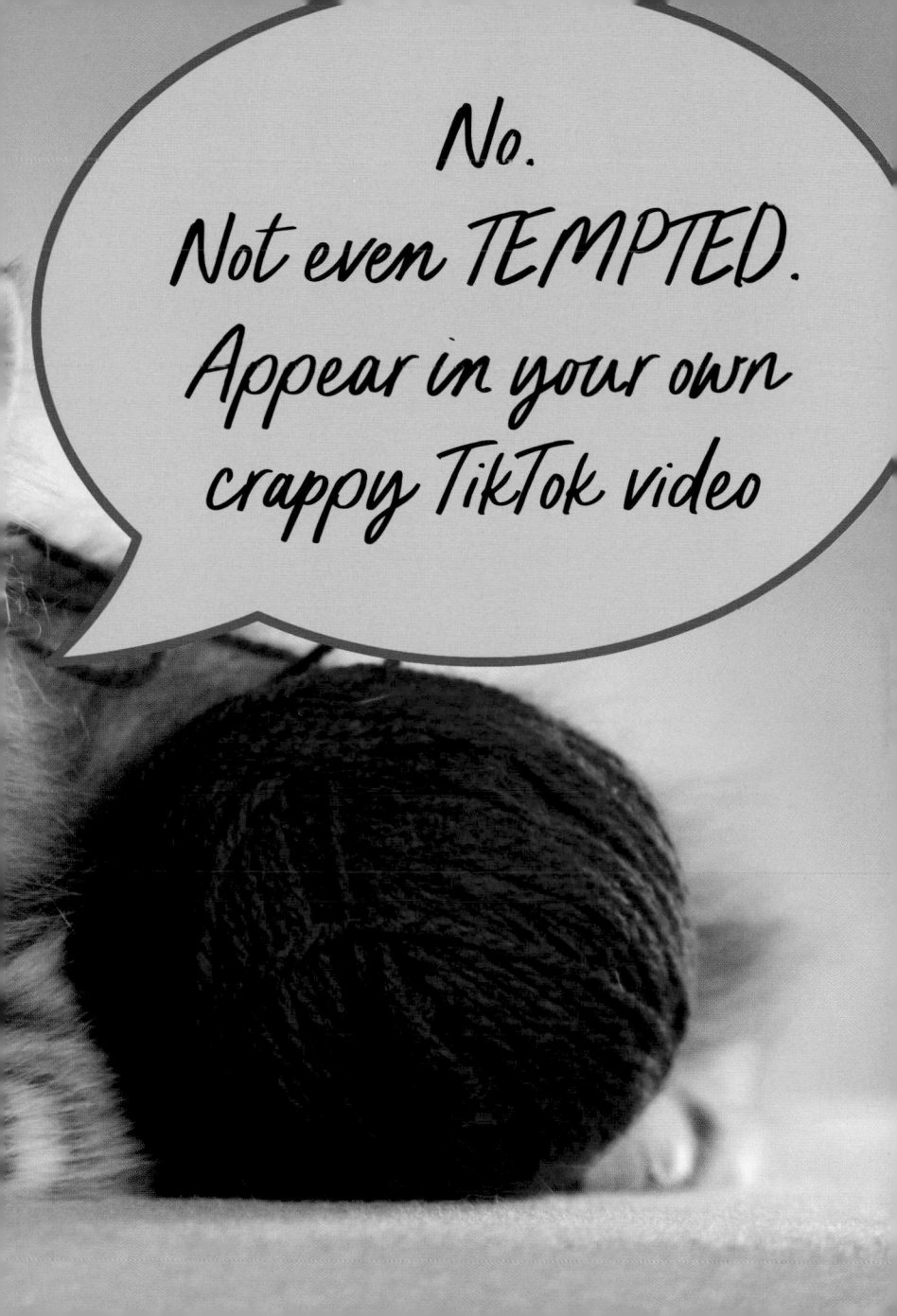
No.
Not even TEMPTED.
Appear in your own
crappy TikTok video

Giddyup Fido! And next time don't forget the SADDLE!

Woo

And none of your fucking backchat or you're off to Battersea!

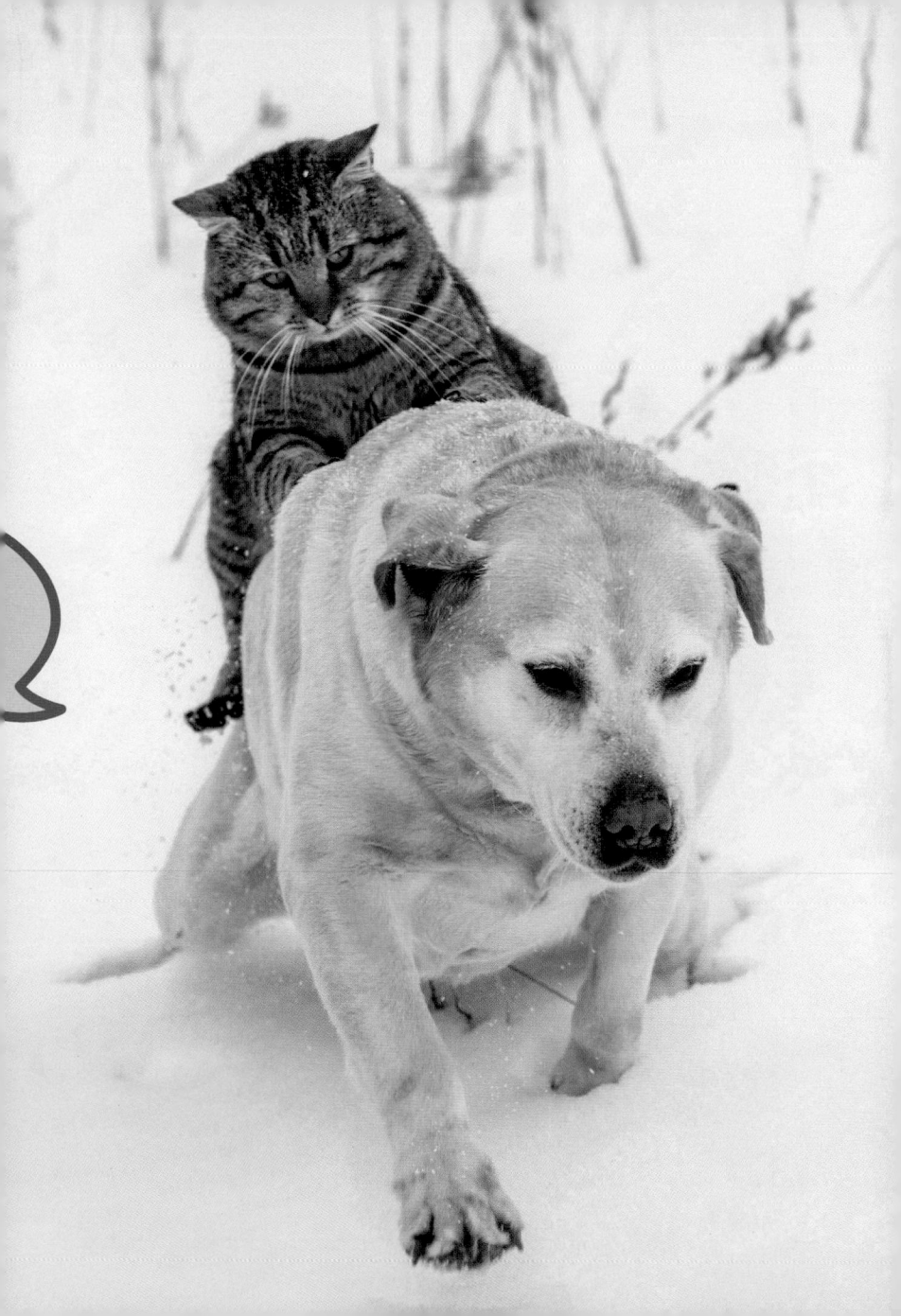

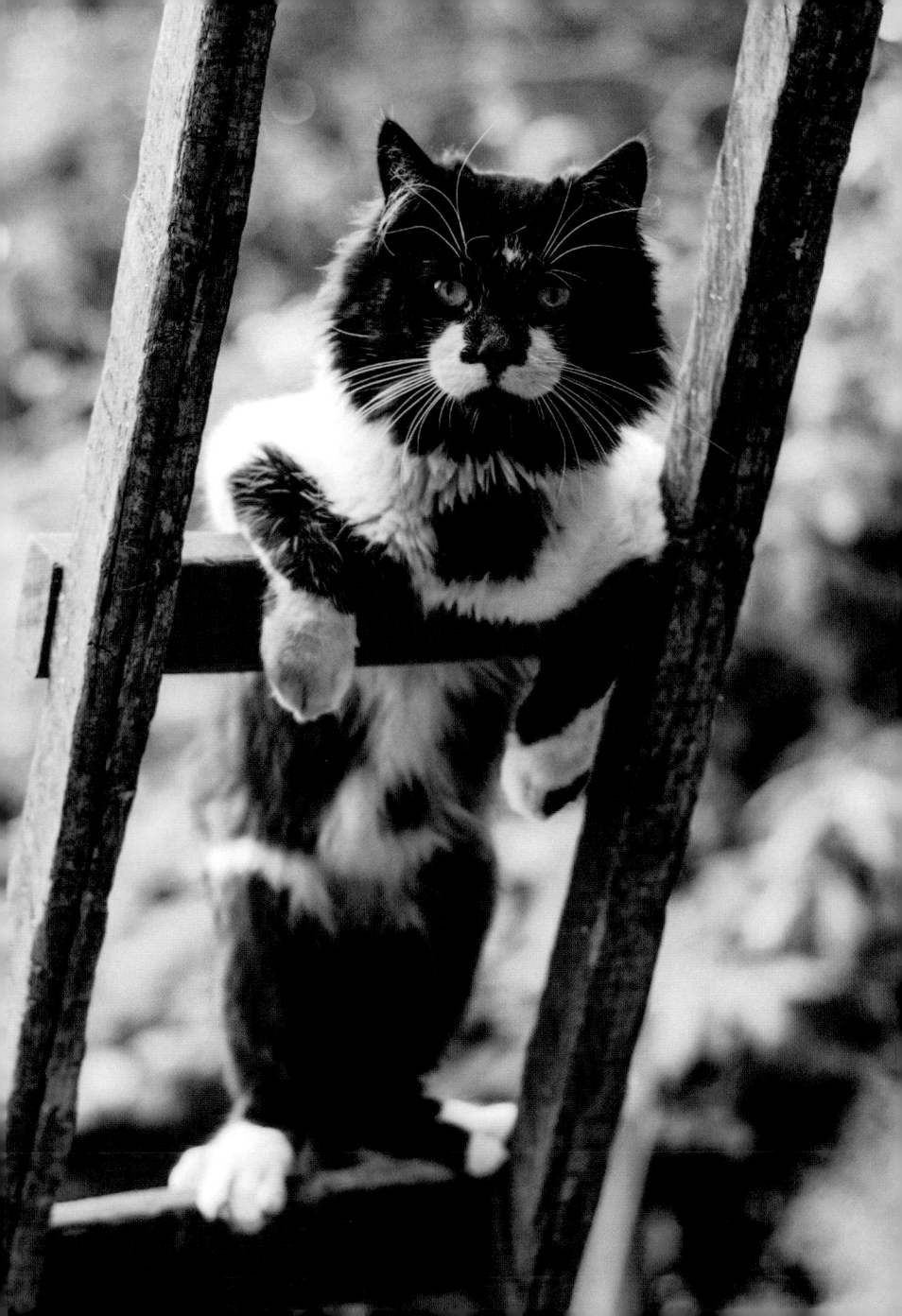

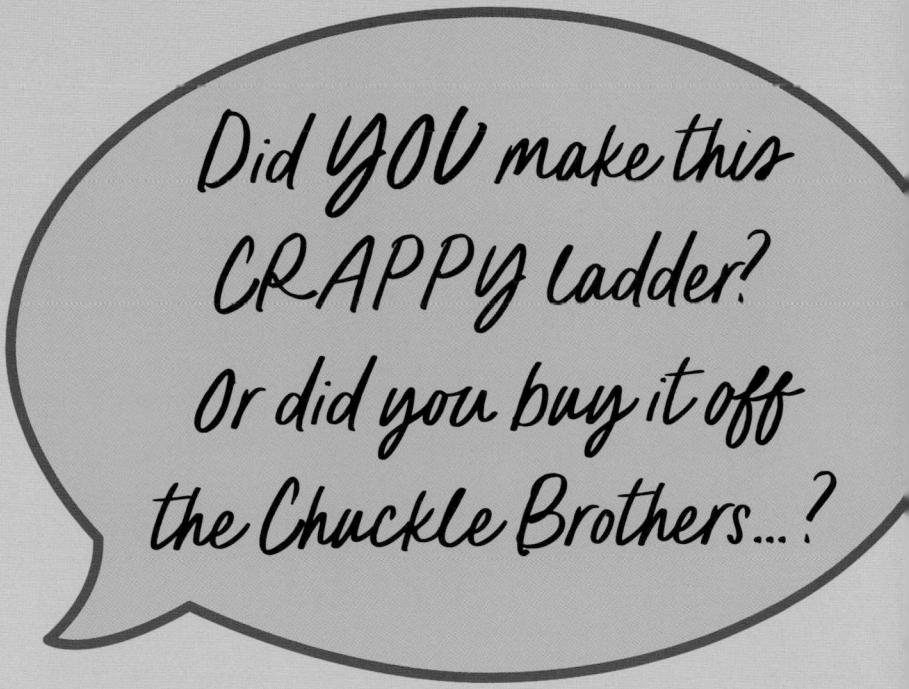
Did YOU make this
CRAPPY ladder?
Or did you buy it off
the Chuckle Brothers...?

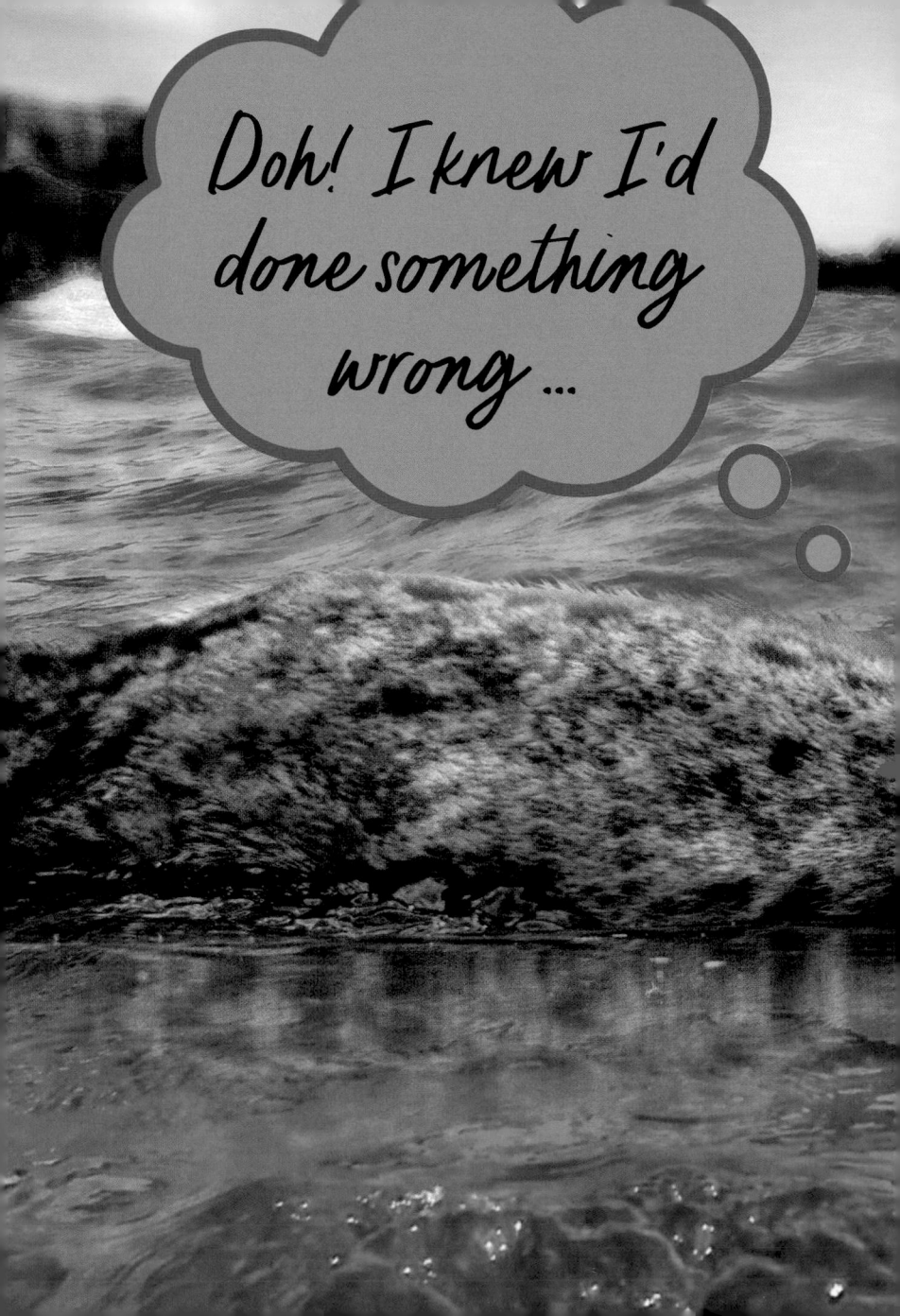
Doh! I knew I'd done something wrong ...

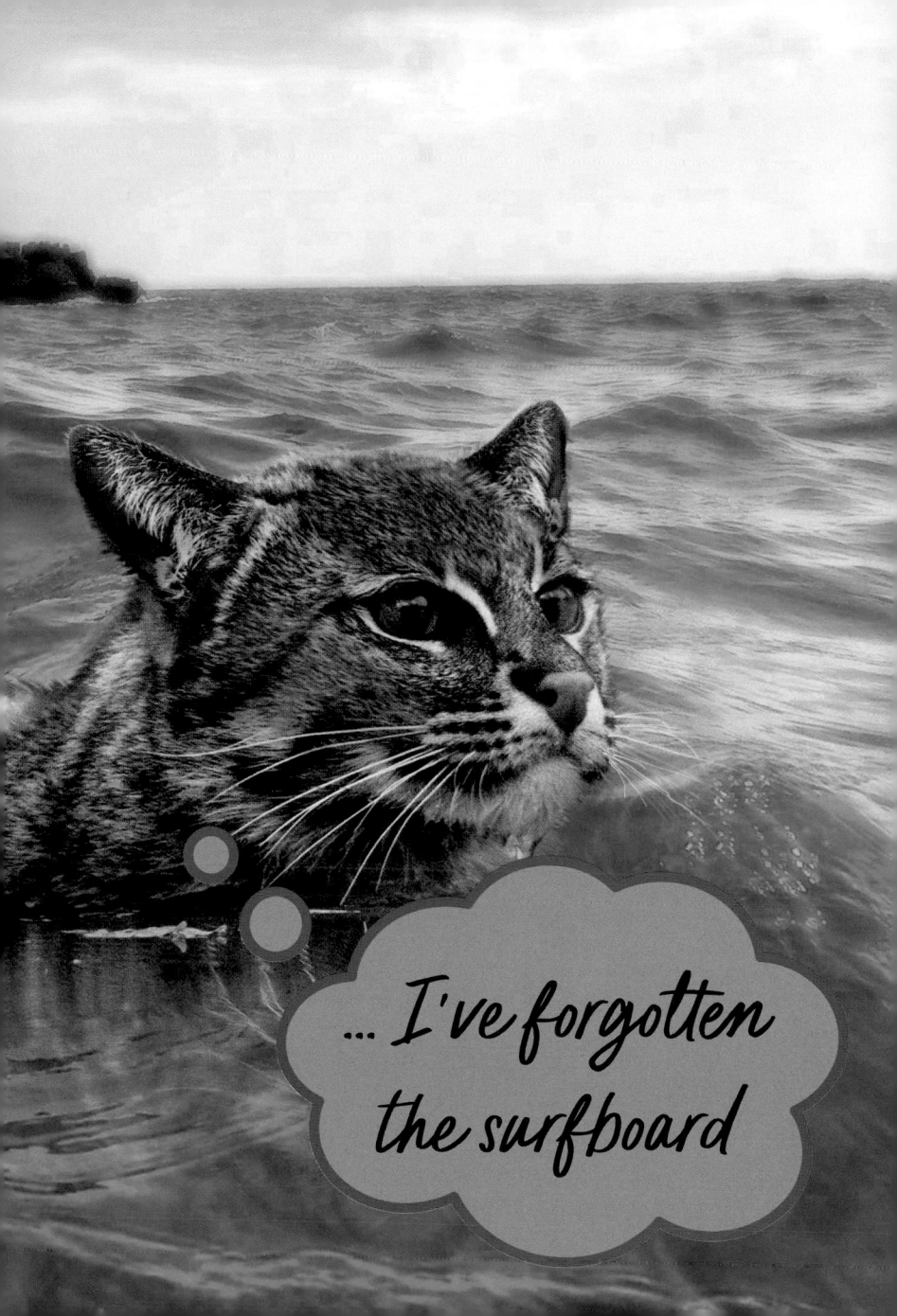
... I've forgotten
the surfboard

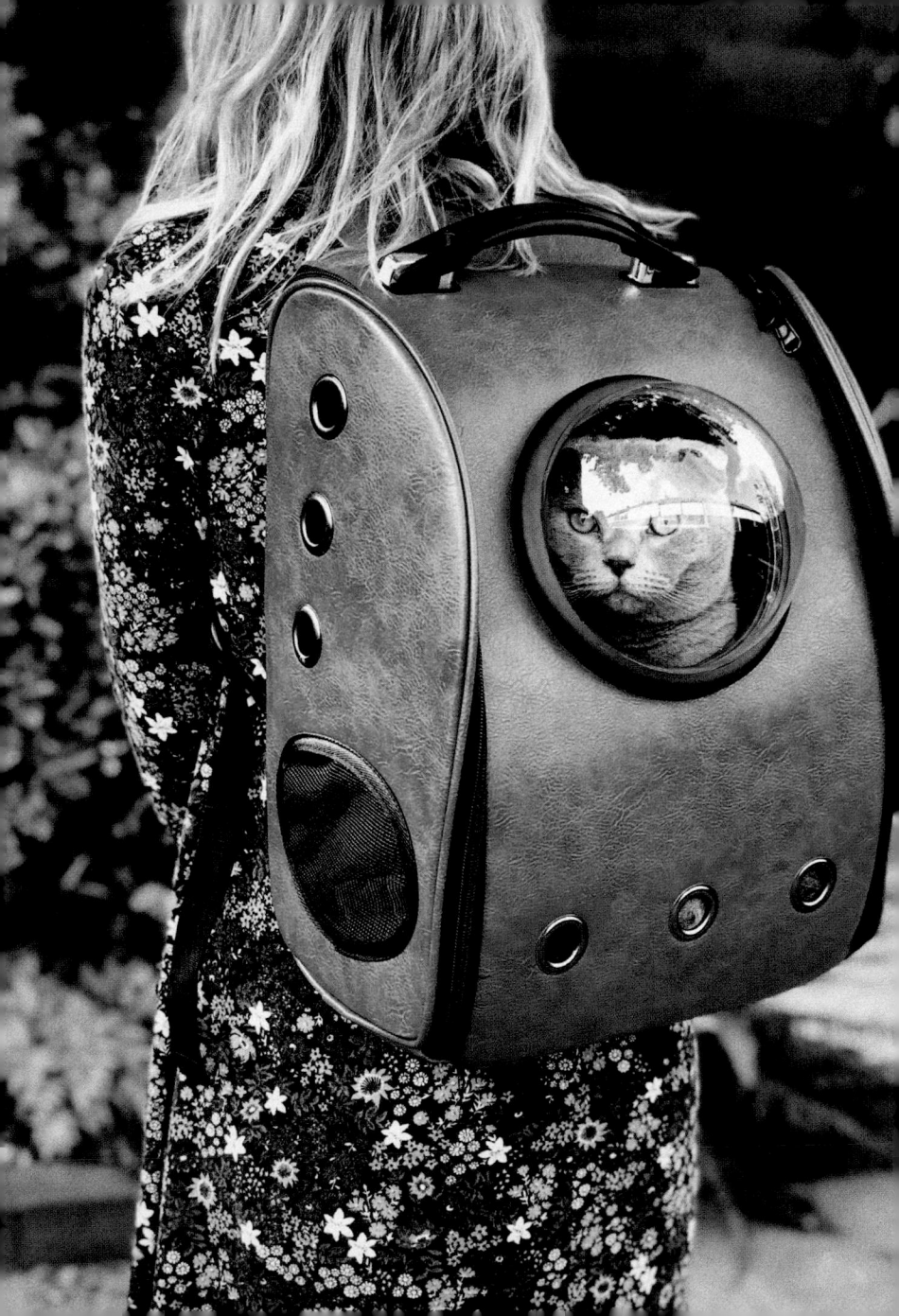

This is Major Tom cat to Ground Control. I'm floating in a most peculiar fucking way ...

Picture Credits

All photos courtesy of Alamy with the exceptions of:
Page 5, Unsplash/Zhang Kaiyv, Page 6, Unsplash/Paul Hanaoka, Page 16, Unsplash/Miron Cristina, Page 21, Unsplash/Marco Biondi, Page 32, Unsplash/Omid Armin, Page 34, Unsplash/Marko Blazevic, Page 38, Unsplash/Jiawei Zhao, Page 41, Unsplash/Rafael Ishkhanyan, Page 42, Unsplash/Tran Mau Tri Tam, Page 45, Unsplash/Karina Vorozheeva, Page 49, Unsplash/Jerry Wang, Page 50, Unsplash/Hannah Reding, Page 59, Getty Images, Page 60, Getty Images, Page 63, Unsplash/Anna-Yenina, Page 64, Getty Images, Page 68, Unsplash/River FX, Page 70, Getty Images, Page 72, Unsplash/Garrett Bear, Page 77, Getty Images, Page 78, Unsplash/Adam Kuylenstierne, Page 81, Unsplash/Marthijn Brinks, Page 82, Unsplash/Marta Munoz, Page 96, Unsplash/Erda Estremera, Page 98, Unsplash/Carlos Deleon, Page 122, Unsplash/Cris Obey, Page 126, Unsplash/Raoul Droog.